LEAD, GUIDE, AND WALK BESIDE

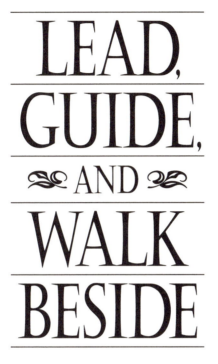

Ardeth Greene Kapp

Deseret Book Company
Salt Lake City, Utah

To my mother,
a leader who had vision,
courage, and faith

Library of Congress Cataloging-in-Publication Data
Kapp, Ardeth Greene, 1931-
    Lead, guide, and walk beside / Ardeth Greene Kapp.
        p.   cm.
    Includes bibliographical references and index.
    ISBN 1-57345-439-7
    1. Mormon women—Religious life.   2. Christian leadership—Church of Jesus Christ of Latter-day Saints.   3. Women in church work—Church of Jesus Christ of Latter-day Saints.   I. Title.
BX8641.K37   1998
248.4'89332'082—dc21   98-35915
                                                                                        CIP

Printed in the United States of America
10   9   8   7   6   5   4   3   2   1   72082 - 6370

CONTENTS

❧

ACKNOWLEDGMENTS

I wish to thank my husband, Heber, for his continued encouragement and support of my writing projects. I'm grateful to Sheri Dew, vice president of publishing at Deseret Book, for initiating the idea for this book, and to Ronald Millett, president, who continues to be a support in my writing efforts. I am indebted to Emily Watts, an excellent editor, and Kent Ware, a most capable designer, for their skills and for the joy it is to work with them. I acknowledge with appreciation the time spent in the initial planning of this work with my dear friend Carolyn Rasmus. I express gratitude for the many mentors and great leaders—men and women—with whom I have had the privilege to associate.

I am humbly and deeply grateful for our Lord and Savior Jesus Christ, the perfect leader, who leads us, guides us, and walks beside us as we strive to follow his example and take part in his work and glory, "to bring to pass the immortality and eternal life of man" (Moses 1:39).

PART ONE

THE VISION

OF

LEADERSHIP

INTRODUCTION

The little stone which was cut out of the mountain
without hands as seen in Daniel's vision is rolling forth
to fill the whole earth. No force under the heavens can
stop it if we will walk in righteousness and be faithful
and true. The Almighty Himself is at our head.

PRESIDENT GORDON B. HINCKLEY, *ENSIGN*, MAY 1995, P. 71

We share a remarkable time in Church history and in the history of the world. As women, we are experiencing a broader concept of leadership than we have known in the past. We are living in a time when our voice, our influence may be far more powerful than ever before—if we are prepared.

President Spencer W. Kimball, speaking to the women of the Church, addressed us with these stirring words: "To be a righteous woman is a glorious thing in any age. To be a righteous woman during the winding-up scenes on this earth, before the second coming of our Savior, is an especially noble calling. The righteous woman's strength and influence today can be tenfold what it might be in more tranquil times" (*My Beloved Sisters* [Salt Lake City: Deseret Book, 1979], p. 17).

Ours is not a tranquil time, as foreseen by the apostle Paul: "This know also, that in the last days perilous times shall come" (2 Timothy 3:1). While the world is darkening in iniquity, and the war that was begun in heaven continues to rage upon the earth, there is an increasing need for the support and strength, the protection and powerful influence of strong families, including ward families and stake families.

Growing up in a small town in Alberta, Canada, I was surrounded by two sets of grandparents, eighteen aunts and uncles, and thirty-three cousins. What a resource for support, encouragement, and direction! Everyone knew what was expected, and all the family members, including the children, were like watchmen on the tower for each other.

In our mobile society, where extended family members often live far away and become a distant support at best, it is increasingly important that ward and stake families are strengthened. We need to work together, to sustain and encourage each other while striving to protect, enrich, and guard the home from the opposition that would, if possible, divide the family, weaken the line, and destroy our safety.

Today in the Church there is an increasing call for men and women to counsel together as we face the advances of the adversary. Elder M. Russell Ballard has written: "Priesthood leaders cannot afford to overlook the experience, wisdom, sensitivity, and insight women bring to such deliberations. . . . [I] encourage priesthood leaders to invite the sisters to more fully participate in developing solutions to the difficult problems confronting members of the Church."

He continues by quoting a statement of President Howard W. Hunter: "It seems to me that there is a great need to rally the women of the Church to stand with and for the Brethren in stemming the tide of evil that surrounds us and in moving forward the work of our Savior. . . . Obedient to him we are a majority. But only together can we accomplish the work he has given us to do and be prepared for the day when we shall see him" (*Counseling with Our Councils* [Salt Lake City: Deseret Book, 1997], p. ix).

For some, men and women both, it may require an adjustment of thought and tradition to include women more actively in leadership decisions. For example, on one occasion when I was traveling with another sister outside the United States on a Church assignment, there was a meeting scheduled for 7:00 P.M. to which all leaders in the stake, men and women, were invited. The General Authority we were traveling with had called the meeting and, of course, would be presiding. The other sister and I had been asked by the presiding authority to do a major portion of the training. It had been announced that two sisters from Salt Lake were coming to make this presentation.

When we arrived, the sisters were all in their places on the front rows of the chapel. The local brethren were mingling together outside the building. When asked about their delay in joining the sisters inside, one of the men, speaking for the others, explained that they understood women would be doing the teaching. It became immediately apparent that these brethren, according to custom and tradition and culture, did not feel comfortable in a training session to be presented by sisters, even though a General Authority was presiding and conducting. They did, however, respond to the direction given. They came into the building and sat on the back rows of the small chapel, separating themselves from the sisters by several rows of benches. These good, dedicated men and women had yet to learn the benefits of uniting and combining their resources in the battle against the influence of the world.

One time, in thoughtful contemplation on this matter, I was reminded of an experience I had had years earlier. It came to me like a parable, to teach a lesson that I have since clung to with conviction, a principle I value beyond words to express. I call it "the parable of the mighty wave."

I was living in California at the time and had been invited shortly after arriving to spend a day at the beach with my friend Elaine. This was a totally new experience for me. It was a glorious day; the weather was perfect. I had been warned about the surf and I recognized the waves to be a powerful force as they washed up on the beach in regular intervals. I thought I was being cautious about not getting out into the water too far. However, I did have some degree of confidence because I had learned as a youth to swim in the river and could even swim upstream against the rapids for a time.

With this confidence, I inched myself little by little, further and further from the shoreline. At one point a huge wave caught me and carried me out into the ocean far beyond my ability to be in control. I struggled with every ounce of energy to swim toward the shore, but after only a little progress I would be pulled back by another powerful wave. This happened again and again. I cannot recall at what point I became too exhausted to continue the struggle, but I will never forget the terrifying feeling I experienced before letting go.

The next thing I knew, I was lying exhausted, facedown, far up on the beach. I had somehow been carried to safety by the force of a mighty wave.

I seldom spoke of this frightening experience for a long time afterward. The fear was so intense that it was uncomfortable to revisit it even in memory. However, this entire episode came back to my mind years later, replayed this time with excitement, a vision, a testimony of what I felt the Lord was wanting me to understand. The message to me was clear: The mighty wave was the power of the priesthood, the power that could carry every lost and struggling soul to safety and would wash them up onto the shore while washing the beach clean—not just once but again and again and again, forever, as long as the ocean existed.

The parable of the mighty wave confirmed for me a true principle. There are some things, like unfounded traditions, that we need to let go of so that men and women counseling together can become a mighty force in rescuing, saving, and bringing souls to safety—unto Christ. As sisters in the auxiliaries, if we let go—not give up or give out, but just let go of some traditions—then we can become a part of the mighty wave. We have been taught by prophets that there is only one organizational channel, and it is the priesthood channel. We need to learn to work effectively within that channel.

I can hear (maybe with some justification) some sisters expressing concern that the opportunity for active participation is not possible with their priesthood leaders. I believe that when sisters are truly prepared, changes will come. These may be changes of attitude or even changes of leaders on the part of both men and women, but seemingly impossible situations can change. Even walls can come down if necessary to accomplish the Lord's work.

The Prophet Joseph Smith understood effective leadership when he made this statement: "I teach the people correct principles and they govern themselves" (quoted by John Taylor in *Journal of Discourses,* 10:57–58). Practices change. Times and circumstances vary. But true principles are universal and eternal in nature. My desire is to present correct leadership principles in hopes of helping us all become more effective in our callings as we lead, guide, and walk beside each other.

These writings are certainly not a scholarly attempt to cover the vast elements of leadership, nor is this work intended to be a textbook for mastering the professional art of leadership. Rather, it has sprung from my conviction that we are approaching a time when women leaders are being invited and expected to become a more powerful influence for good in the Church and in the world. We are experiencing increased opportunities for men and women to work interdependently on behalf of individuals and families, to reach out to others who might be carried to safety by the "mighty wave."

When I was serving at Church headquarters, we held a meeting to which one of our priesthood leaders, a General Authority, came unexpectedly. He had no specific purpose for being there, other than to lend support. However, it turned into a great teaching moment when, at the conclusion of the meeting, he said: "You realize, sisters, that while you are entrusted with the responsibilities relating to this call for an indefinite period of time, you are having a rich and wonderful opportunity to learn, practice, and develop leadership skills that you will draw from in years to come in a variety of callings, not only here but throughout all eternity." After that concept was opened to our minds, we had a better understanding of why it is so important to learn and practice leadership skills in a variety of settings while we have the opportunity.

The stories, illustrations, and examples in this book are

true. They come from an accumulation of experiences and lessons I have learned from the many great leaders with whom I have been blessed to associate over the years. Although I acknowledge emphatically that this publication is not in any way intended to be an official statement on leadership for women in the Church, it is hoped that in every detail it will be found to be supportive of and consistent with the direction from authorized ward, stake, and general leaders to whom we look for direction. For this reason I wish to include a statement presented by the First Presidency and the Quorum of the Twelve in the document "Leadership Training Emphasis," which provides the following guidelines:

"Families—Teach the preeminence of the home and family as the basic organizational unit of the Church. Encourage each family member, parents and children, to study the scriptures, pray regularly, and follow the example of the Savior in all things.

"Adults—Encourage each adult to be worthy to receive the ordinances of the temple. Teach all adults to identify their ancestors and perform sacred temple ordinances for them.

"Youth—Help prepare each young man to receive the Melchizedek Priesthood, to receive the ordinances of the temple, and to be worthy to serve a full-time mission. Help prepare each young woman to be worthy to make and keep sacred covenants and receive the ordinances of the temple.

"All Members—Leaders, members, and stake and full-time missionaries work cooperatively in a balanced effort to help convert, retain, and activate our Heavenly Father's children. Teach members to provide for themselves, their families, and the poor and the needy in the Lord's way."

Elder M. Russell Ballard adds this emphasis: "These are the things that matter. These are the things that will make a positive difference in people's lives. And these are the things that should be the focus and objective of every presiding council in the Church as we seek to join the Lord in his work and his glory—'to bring to pass the immortality and eternal life of man' (Moses 1:39)" (*Counseling with Our Councils,* p. 77). It is to this end that I desire to contribute in some small way to the dedicated efforts of leaders striving to help build the kingdom.

CHAPTER ONE

WOMEN LEADERS AND PRIESTHOOD AUTHORITY

*I will pour out my spirit upon all flesh; and your sons
and your daughters shall prophesy, your old men shall
dream dreams, your young men shall see visions:
and also upon the servants and upon the handmaids
in those days will I pour out my spirit.*

JOEL 2:28-29

President Gordon B. Hinckley has urged all members of the
Church: "Stand strong, even to become a leader in speaking up in behalf of those causes which make our civilization
shine and which give comfort and peace to our lives. You can
be a leader. You must be a leader, as a member of this Church,
in those causes for which the Church stands" (*Church News,*
September 21, 1996, p. 3). This challenge is extended to
women as well as men in these latter days.

Can you imagine the emotion that could mount in a discussion about women leaders and men in authority in the climate of our society today? In the world, there will continue to
be confusion about men's and women's roles, but in the
Church, eternal principles are in place that clarify our responsibilities and provide order, opportunity, and direction. As
Elder Dallin H. Oaks explains, "The Lord's servants must do
the Lord's work in the Lord's way or their efforts will come to
naught" (*The Lord's Way* [Salt Lake City: Deseret Book, 1991],
p. 5). The Lord's way calls for men and women to be directed
by priesthood authority and to receive inspiration from the
same source.

In the Church there are many resources available when we understand priesthood authority and Church government. I believe the brethren are looking to the women of the Church to study and understand the doctrine of the priesthood. Elder James E. Talmage explained: "It is not given to woman to exercise the authority of the Priesthood independently; nevertheless, in the sacred endowments associated with the ordinances pertaining to the House of the Lord, woman shares with man the blessings of the Priesthood" (*Young Woman's Journal,* October 1914, p. 602).

From the writings of Brigham Young we read, "The Priesthood of the Son of God, which we have in our midst, is a perfect order and system of government, and this alone can deliver the human family from all the evils which now afflict its members, and insure them happiness and felicity hereafter" (*Discourses of Brigham Young,* comp. John A. Widtsoe [Salt Lake City: Deseret Book, 1975], p. 130). "There is no act of a Latter-day Saint," he said another time, "no duty required—no time given, exclusive and independent of the Priesthood. Everything is subject to it, whether preaching, business, or any other act pertaining to the proper conduct of this life" (*Discourses of Brigham Young,* p. 133).

I learned the hard way that when we fail to utilize the proper channels of priesthood authority, we can handicap our efforts. Years ago I was called and set apart as a Laurel adviser. I was young. It was not my first calling in the Church, but it was the first time I remember having such a compelling desire to magnify my calling. My little class of twelve girls decided to have a fashion show to raise money for our stake building project. We even got Rose Marie Reid, a nationally renowned fashion designer who was a member of the Church, to agree to come and narrate our little show.

As the word spread, the project became bigger than we had ever expected. It was the first time I realized that to talk is easy, but to organize, plan, lead, manage, and succeed in accomplishing what you want to have happen is far more demanding. With more questions than I had answers for, and more people than we had room for, and more responsibility than I had experience for, I felt for the first time the heavy weight, the load that accompanies leadership. I was in over my head.

It was then that I went to my Heavenly Father in earnest prayer. I went out into a secluded spot in nature and there poured out my heart. Not having cleared the project or even discussed the plan through the proper procedure, I accepted full responsibility. "Father in Heaven," I pleaded, "if you will just see me through this crisis so the young women will not be disappointed and the guests will not be dissatisfied and the bishop will not be unhappy with me, I promise I will never get myself involved in anything of this magnitude again."

Our Father in Heaven heard the prayer of this fledgling leader. The fashion show was a great success; it was even written up in the *Church News*. But I learned from that hard lesson, years ago, that it is not intended that we carry the load of leadership alone—not in the Church, in the home, or anywhere.

Although the work of the Lord is always subject to priesthood direction, the heavens are not closed to women as long as our hearts are open to the Spirit. The prophet Joel recorded the promise of the Lord: "I will pour out my spirit upon all flesh; and your sons and your daughters shall prophesy . . . your young men shall see visions: and also upon the servants and upon the handmaids in those days will I pour out my spirit" (Joel 2:28-29). I bear testimony of this promise. More is required of us as women than to simply "wait in some backroom" until called upon.

If there is any question about the worth of a righteous woman's influence, her value, and her insights, consider the words of President Hinckley to the women of the Church: "I feel to invite women everywhere to rise to the great potential within you. I do not ask that you reach beyond your capacity. I hope you will not nag yourselves with thoughts of failure. I hope you will not try to set goals far beyond your capacity to achieve. I hope you will simply do what you can do in the best way you know. If you do so, you will witness miracles come to pass" (*Teachings of Gordon B. Hinckley* [Salt Lake City: Deseret Book, 1997], p. 696).

Today, as in times past, women shoulder responsibilities for the mission of the Church. President Spencer W. Kimball said: "Much of the major growth that is coming to the Church in the last days will come because many of the good women of the world (in whom there is often such an inner sense of spirituality) will be drawn to the Church in large numbers. This will happen to the degree that the women of the Church reflect righteousness and articulateness in their lives and to the degree that they are seen as distinct and different—in happy ways—from the women of the world. . . . Thus it will be that the female exemplars of the Church will be a significant force in both the numerical and the spiritual growth of the Church in the last days" (*My Beloved Sisters* [Salt Lake City: Deseret Book, 1979], pp. 44–45).

When we as women attune our ears to the words of prophets as from the voice of the Lord himself (see D&C 1:38), we are lifted, elevated, and magnified in our possibilities and opportunities. From our homes will come children who have been nurtured and prepared as leaders for generations to come. There is nowhere that our influence is more important to the Lord's work than in our homes, but it must not stop there. A righteous woman's influence extends beyond the home.

LEADERSHIP IN CHURCH CALLINGS

Consider this statement from President Hinckley as we attempt to place a value on the contribution that can be made by women: "What a resource are the women of The Church of Jesus Christ of Latter-day Saints. . . . You bring a measure of wholeness to us. You have great strength. With dignity and tremendous ability, you carry forward the remarkable programs of the Relief Society, the Young Women, and the

Primary. You teach Sunday School. We walk at your side as your companions and your brethren with respect and love, with honor and great admiration. It was the Lord who designated that men in His Church should hold the priesthood. It was He who has given you your capabilities to round out this great and marvelous organization, which is the Church and kingdom of God" (*Ensign,* November 1996, p. 70).

Because the Lord directs his work in heaven and on earth through the priesthood, sometimes sisters may abdicate their responsibility to fully magnify their callings because they interpret "loyalty to the priesthood" to mean that they should simply take direction from those in authority. Some use the term *priesthood* interchangeably to speak of priesthood power, authority, and holders of the priesthood, and may not accept responsibility for receiving inspiration and helping to advance the work by speaking up.

On the other hand, there are those in authority, bearers of the priesthood, who may not understand the place of women leaders called by priesthood authority and so do not benefit from the power and blessing of a united effort. This must not be. Understanding priesthood is a blessing to both men and women.

I learned something of my responsibility in relation to the priesthood in one of my first meetings with the Presiding Bishopric over twenty years ago as a counselor in the Young Women general presidency. I was new in my calling and felt somewhat overwhelmed as we approached that meeting. I had a certain responsibility that was to be an item on that day's agenda. I waited anxiously with pen in hand to receive any direction, prepared to follow without question. I spoke briefly to the matter when called upon and then waited for Bishop Brown's response. He listened, paused, leaned forward in his chair with his hands folded on the table in front of him, and then asked, "Ardeth, in view of what you have presented, what is your recommendation?" At that time in my experience I had never anticipated that the Presiding Bishop of the Church would ask for my recommendation. This was a daunting responsibility.

I was anxious and nervous and felt the weight of my calling. Just at that time my nephew Kent, on his second day of kindergarten, told his mom he had pains in his stomach and didn't want to go to school. Before trying to resolve the problem, she determined to uncover, if possible, the cause. "Kent," she asked, "what are you feeling?" He explained his concern very clearly. "Mom," he cried, "I'm afraid of the hard work and the big boys." I thought I could relate to his feelings in a strange sort of way.

A young sister who had recently been called as ward Relief Society president had similar concerns. "I am much younger than most of the sisters in my ward," she told me. "I am inexperienced. How do I do it?" She might have asked, as others have, "How do I honor and sustain priesthood leaders, and how do I contribute so I will be heard? How can I be courageous and bold, but not overbearing?"

These questions are familiar to many women called to positions of leadership. Should a woman leader interpret "supporting the priesthood" to mean going along with a plan she has concerns over without expressing her views? I think not. Leadership requires studying, preparing, seeking, asking. Inspiration is available to those called to lead—women as well as men—when we seek it earnestly, ask prayerfully, and work diligently. And having prepared in mind and heart, we speak up in the spirit of the work.

We read in the scriptures that if we are prepared we shall not fear (see D&C 38:30). Brigham Young explained, "If you want the mind and will of God . . . get it, it is just as much your privilege as of any other member of the Church and Kingdom of God. It is your privilege and duty to live so that you know when the word of the Lord is spoken to you and when the mind of the Lord is revealed to you. I say it is your duty to live so as to know and understand all these things" (*Discourses of Brigham Young*, p. 163).

MEN AND WOMEN WORKING TOGETHER

It is not a new discovery that men and women think differently and see things differently and respond to life differently. We are supposed to. The insights, unique perspectives, experience, and points of view of both men and women are needed to accomplish the work. We need to understand our differences as being complementary and unifying, not divisive and separating.

One area of difference became obvious to me in comparing men's and women's journal entries. When I was sixteen years old, my father was serving as bishop, and one night six young missionaries came to our home to stay overnight before leaving for their field of labor miles away. Following that memorable occasion, I took to my journal and wrote pages and pages with all the details of an Elder Kapp, who had been one of the six elders. Years later, at the first opportunity, I searched his journal to discover what he had written of that historic occasion. Finally I came upon the page and read these words: "Met the bishop's daughter and she is cute and fun but kind of young." Even allowing for the fact that he was an obedient missionary focused on his work, this seemed to be a rather brief report of the experience. Just the bottom line, so to speak.

We have in our family the separate journals of my grandfather and grandmother, describing how they left Utah in a wagon with their young family and headed north to Canada. Reading their individual accounts of the same day, one would wonder in many cases if in fact they were on the same journey. Their accounts were so different—yet they were equally significant.

Of course, there will be occasions when men and women won't see eye to eye, for whatever reason. There may be occasions when the opportunity to express one's recommendations is not made available. But how we respond to priesthood leaders can have a tremendous influence, I believe, on our opportunities to participate, to be heard, to learn from others, and to contribute. In conversation with some priesthood leaders, I have learned about men's natural reactions to certain leadership styles and how their responses can be influenced.

The first illustration is that of a woman who is overbearing and difficult to work with, maybe a person full of "zeal without knowledge," as Brother Hugh Nibley speaks of. (I don't know anyone like that, do you?) The instinctive reaction of other leaders would be to minimize or even avoid any interaction with this leader.

The second illustration is the woman who is passive and does not contribute. It is almost as though she were invisible. The reaction is to ignore her and expect nothing from her.

The third illustration is the leader who sees her role too narrowly, too stereotypically. She seems as fragile and delicate as a porcelain doll. The reaction of other leaders is patronizing and overprotective; they might put her on a pedestal and thereby limit her growth.

The fourth leader is the sister who is very team oriented, shares a joint stewardship, and participates as a co-leader whose contributions are vital. She is well prepared and speaks up. She works with others interdependently and synergistically. The reaction from other leaders is to actively solicit her counsel and help.

It would be wise, I believe, for us to take a reading occasionally on our leadership style and consider the degree to which we are all responsible for the working relationship we have with other leaders. We need not think and feel the way others do to have our contributions be of value. We don't all need to see things the same way to maintain good relations. But we need to be sensitive to how our behavior affects other people, and make changes when appropriate.

Of course, even in the best of circumstances, things don't always work out the way we might wish. I recall one meeting with our priesthood leaders when I left the room feeling somewhat discouraged, misunderstood, and a bit annoyed. Walking past a plant in the hallway, without thinking I reached out in frustration and hit one of the leaves on the plant. Have you ever been that frustrated or discouraged? Let me tell you there is a lesson to learn in every situation. The very next day, when I passed that plant in the hallway—you may not believe this, but the whole plant was wilted and had turned brown. It appeared dead. Someone must have forgotten to water it, but the timing was perfect for the lesson. I paused in amazement. The plant seemed to say to me, "If you become discouraged you will kill the Spirit within, and if you lose the Spirit, the life needed to sustain you as a leader will soon die."

Following this experience, the sister who was with me on that occasion would from time to time smile and say, "Now remember, don't hit the plant." It has been a good reminder in times of frustration. I would caution against our ever succumbing to the influence of the adversary by allowing a feeling of discouragement, resentment, criticism, or offense to creep in. It helps no one if we harbor resentment or hurt because our ideas are not readily accepted. Negative feelings, if allowed to smolder, can be destructive to the Spirit. Remember the message of the wilted plant: we can lose the life and light that come from the Spirit if we are not mindful. Refusing to be offended when things may not go our way will protect against the destructive influence of the adversary.

There may be, unfortunately, circumstances when the opportunity to be heard is not made available. Even being heard is not necessarily the same as being understood. An example given by Elder M. Russell Ballard offers insight into how we might work more effectively.

Elder Ballard tells of a stake presidency who went into a priesthood executive committee meeting to tell the brethren how a seminar for temple preparation could be held. They described the meeting, "They [the brethren] just sat there, listening to us, without any expressions of support or excitement." In their next presidency meeting, the stake presidency counseled together on how the situation could be improved. In the president's words: "It occurred to us that we had the habit of telling the high council how we were going to do things, as opposed to counseling with them and receiving their ideas and input. At our next priesthood executive committee meeting we approached the temple preparation seminar in a different way. We asked for their suggestions and recommendations, and then we sat back and waited for them to respond. At first they were hesitant—this was a new way of doing things. But soon momentum began to build and the ideas began to flow. . . . After the meeting, one of the brethren came up to me and said, 'This is one of the most productive meetings I have ever attended'" (*Counseling with Our Councils* [Salt Lake City: Deseret Book, 1997], p. 85). Surely the same principles would apply to an auxiliary presidency presenting an idea to a bishopric or stake council, or even a parent working in a family council.

I am reminded of a time when as a general Young Women presidency our preparation time had been lengthy—months long, including counseling with our priesthood leaders on what we knew were some of the weightier matters of our calling. It wasn't the style of the jewelry or the size of the manual or the color of the flags that consumed our thoughts or took our time. Those things are nice and, yes, important, but must not be confused with the weightier matters.

The time arrived for the final presentation. But we worried (having invested so much) about being closed minded or biased in our opinions and thus not receptive to further counsel from our priesthood leaders. We knelt in prayer prior to the meeting and asked, "If this proposal is right, may the ears of our priesthood leaders be open, but if not, let them be closed, that we may not go amiss."

At the conclusion of the presentation, which was well received, as we prepared to leave, one of the priesthood leaders thanked us for our work and said, "Today, sisters, you have opened not only our eyes but also our ears." This statement by one who had not been aware of our earlier prayer was a witness to us that we had been directed by the Spirit in weighty matters.

President Hinckley has spoken of what we know to be the weightier matters: "When all is said and done, our greatest responsibility as leaders in this Church is to increase the knowledge of our people concerning their place as sons and daughters of God, their divine inheritance and their divine, eternal destiny" (*Teachings of Gordon B. Hinckley,* p. 117). Without strong leaders, how can the "weightier matters" be conveyed to congregations new in the faith? And how are those leadership qualities to be developed worldwide?

Responsible leadership requires thinking. In the mission field I would occasionally ask the missionaries, "Ere you left your room this morning, did you think to pray? And when you prayed, did you stop to think?" Thinking, pondering, and praying are all part of the preparation for our leadership responsibilities, and a woman's voice, when lifted in the spirit of her calling, places her in a position to be valued, to contribute, and to make a difference.

Consider these compelling words of President Boyd K. Packer, speaking to the women of the Church in a general conference: "We need women who will applaud decency and quality in everything from the fashion of clothing to crucial social issues. We need women who are organized and women who can organize. We need women with executive ability who can plan and direct and administer; women who can teach, women who can speak out. There is a great need for women who can receive inspiration to guide them personally in their teaching and in their leadership responsibilities. We need women with the gift of discernment who can view the trends in the world and detect those that, however popular, are shallow or dangerous. We need women who can discern those positions that may not be popular at all, but are right" (*Ensign,* November 1978, p. 8).

I think of Eliza R. Snow, of whom Joseph F. Smith said, "She walked not in the borrowed light of others but faced the morning unafraid and invincible." There are many Eliza R. Snows among us today, and there can be many more. The Lord's way is not to limit opportunity but to expand it just as fast as we are ready. Our contribution as sisters is essential to building the kingdom.

If there is ever a time when women leaders question their value, their worth, and the importance of their contribution, let the words of President Hinckley resonate loud and clear: "I invite every one of you, wherever you may be as members of this church, to stand on your feet and with a song in your heart move forward, living the gospel, loving the Lord, and building the kingdom. Together we shall stay the course and keep the faith, the Almighty being our strength" (*Ensign,* November 1995, p. 72).

This call from a prophet of God is for each one of us, not for someone else. It is for now, according to our circumstances, not later. The call is for you and for me, for our voice, our influence, our goodness. Do you hear the call in your heart and in your mind? In our leadership responsibilities, beginning in our homes, I testify that Christ will lift us up beyond our natural abilities to accomplish our work—which is, in reality, his work.

CHAPTER TWO

A LEADER WITH VISION

Where there is no vision, the people perish.
PROVERBS 29:18

A leader with vision is like a light in the darkness. A leader with vision can motivate people to do things they would not otherwise do, turning dreams into reality by effectively enlisting others in a good cause. To have vision is to be future oriented and to see and believe in something that, with the help of others, you can make happen. It is to move into the unknown with faith, not fear, because of what you see and feel in your mind and heart. Your own vision and conviction can help others begin to see, feel, and believe in what is yet to be realized.

Vision provides the reason for doing some things and for leaving some things undone. Vision provides a basis for planning, setting priorities, and eliminating unnecessary efforts extended on wasteful activities.

President Gordon B. Hinckley admonishes us: "Keep before you the big picture, for this cause is as large as all mankind and as broad as all eternity. This is the church and kingdom of God. It requires the strength, the loyalty, the faith of all if it is to roll forward to bless the lives of our Father's children over the earth. . . .

"President Harold B. Lee once said from this pulpit, quoting an unknown writer, 'Survey large fields and cultivate small ones.' My interpretation of that statement is that we ought to recognize something of the breadth and depth and height—grand and wonderful, large and all-encompassing—of the program of the Lord, and then work with diligence to meet our responsibility for our assigned portion of that program"

(*Teachings of Gordon B. Hinckley* [Salt Lake City: Deseret Book, 1997], p. 431).

Consider the vision given to the young women of the Church when the current Young Women theme and values were presented in a satellite broadcast on November 11, 1985. Can you see in your mind's eye what those Young Women leaders saw at that time? Can you catch the vision?

"To every young woman throughout the entire Church, in every corner of every land: you are important, each one of you. . . . We call upon you and reach out to you, because we have an urgent message for you. In order to receive that message, would you imagine with us for a moment? Would you picture yourself standing with us at the seashore looking out over the mighty ocean? From the beach we can feel the ocean breeze and hear the cry of the birds. We can see the waves break one after the other as they reach the shore. But look with us beyond the breakers and far out to sea. We can see the crest of a great wave forming. . . . We see a wave forming that will move across the earth, reaching every continent and every shore. We call upon you to stand with us, to prepare to take your place in a great forward movement among the young women of the Church—a movement of renewed commitment, a movement in which you are destined to shape history and participate in the fulfillment of prophecy" (Ardeth Kapp, *Stand Up, Lead Out* [Salt Lake City: Deseret Book, 1990], pp. 1–2).

Note that after the vision is shared, there is an invitation for involvement and an expression of confidence in those who would participate in the realization of the vision. A leader with vision will share that vision with others, invite them to become involved, and encourage them along the way.

With a clear vision in mind of what is to be accomplished, we become committed to the cause. Without vision and commitment, when things become difficult we may lose sight of the goal and give up.

I've always been impressed with the story of Florence Chadwick, a swimmer who at thirty-four years of age determined to be the first woman to swim the twenty-two miles from Catalina Island to the California coast. She had already been the first woman to swim the English Channel in both directions.

The day she made the attempt, the California coastline was obscured in dense fog. Her mother and her trainer were at her side in a boat, warding off sharks several times with rifles and encouraging her along. After fifteen hours, she asked to be taken out of the water, but her problem wasn't so much fatigue as it was the bone-chilling cold of the ocean. Though she knew she must be near land, all she could see when she looked toward the shoreline was the thick fog. She stayed with it for a while longer, but near the sixteen-hour mark she was finally lifted, exhausted and freezing, into the boat. It turned out she had given up only half a mile from her goal. "Look, I'm not excusing myself," she told one reporter, "but if I could have just seen land I might have made it."

In a position of leadership, we deal with plenty of sharks and a lot of fog and fatigue and sometimes chilling cold. Leadership is not always popular or comfortable, but once we have the vision of what we want to have happen and are committed to a realization of that mission, we can overcome great obstacles.

We read in Proverbs 29:18, "Where there is no vision, the people perish." I believe we perish when we lose the Spirit, when we lose faith in why we are doing what we are doing. A leader might ask herself, "What is the state of my vision: foggy, vague, and unsure, or clear, specific, and committed?" As leaders in the Church, we all share the same long-range vision of what it is we want to have happen. It is ultimately the same as what our Father in Heaven wants to have happen. We are given a vision of his work, which is also our work, through the Lord speaking to Moses: "For behold, this is my work and my glory—to bring to pass the immortality and eternal life of man" (Moses 1:39). With this long-range vision in mind, it becomes relevant in our individual leadership responsibilities to ask ourselves, "Will this decision, this objective, this plan, this activity contribute to moving us from where we are to where we want to be? Will this effort move us toward or away from the ultimate goal?" An illustration to help clarify this principle might be represented as follows:

Things As They Are	Our Work(→)	Vision
Individual problems	→	Strengthened testimonies
Fog (lack of vision)	→	The Spirit's guide
Cold (lack of spirit)	→	Enthusiasm for life
Sharks (fear)	→	Faith
Fatigue (lack of commitment)	→	Dedication
Inactivity	→	Full participation

Our work is to move things as they are toward things as they can become. Without the proper vision, we might be busily engaged, actively involved, but going in circles—never decreasing that gap. The principle of leading with vision should apply to everything we do. A leader with vision sees the land, not the fog, and has a clear sense of direction and purpose. Though we may not always see the end from the beginning, we go "to the edge of the light," and when we get there, our vision—guided by the Spirit—will extend into the unknown.

GETTING THE VISION

Where does this great vision of our work come from? How can we catch it and hold it in our hearts? Consider the lesson to be learned in the account of Father Lehi and his sons. Lehi was a visionary man and an obedient man. He was given a vision to take his family and depart into the wilderness. He knew what he needed to do. Nephi had a great desire to see what his father had seen, so he asked. "I did cry unto the Lord," he said, "and behold he did visit me" (1 Nephi 2:16). In answer to his prayer, he was blessed to "believe all the words which had been spoken by [his] father." He had not only the direction but the vision. Laman and Lemuel, not having the Spirit or the faith to ask, were of a different nature. Later Nephi posed the question, "Have ye inquired of the Lord? And they said unto me: We have not; for the Lord maketh no such thing known unto us" (1 Nephi 15:8–9).

If we are to get the vision, we must remember the instructions Nephi gave to his brothers: "Do ye not remember the things which the Lord hath said?–If ye will not harden your hearts, and ask me in faith, believing that ye shall receive, with diligence in keeping my commandments, surely these things shall be made known unto you" (1 Nephi 15:11). This invitation is for all of us as we seek for vision concerning our responsibilities as leaders in the Church.

Alma had a similar experience regarding the things of the Spirit: "Behold, I say unto you they are made known unto me by the Holy Spirit of God. Behold, I have fasted and prayed many days that I might know these things of myself. And now I do know of myself that they are true; for the Lord God hath made them manifest unto me by his Holy Spirit; and this is the spirit of revelation which is in me" (Alma 5:46). President Hinckley invites us: "Ask the Lord to lead you by His quiet voice in the things you ought to do as leaders in this Church. You have a great responsibility for the well-being, even the salvation of others. You are very important in this Church. The kind of help you really need won't come from the handbook, though you need to know the handbook; but you'll get the best help from private and thoughtful communion with the Lord. We all need to quietly and calmly reflect on the things of God" (*Teachings of Gordon B. Hinckley*, p. 305).

Effective leaders have a clear vision of what they want to accomplish in their callings. Guidelines, principles, and handbooks help, but the most important thing we can do is inquire of the Lord. In the words of President Wilford Woodruff, "We cannot do the work which God through us intends to have done, unless we place ourselves under His care and direction, and take the sentiment, 'The Kingdom of God, or nothing,' for our motto, as well as the end and aim of our life" (*Journal of Discourses,* 24:51). There is nothing we do to help build the kingdom that is unimportant, and everything we do as leaders in this church is to that end.

SHARING THE VISION

A visionary leader will help others see what she sees, hear what she hears, and feel what she feels. When we share the vision, we inspire others with the real purpose—the "grand why." There are many reasons why we do some things and not others, but the "grand why" is to serve people, reach people, bless people, and bring souls unto Christ.

The work of the adversary is to destroy the Lord's plan. Consider the famous Nazi death camp of Auschwitz, where so many were murdered because of a powerful and influential leader. I am told that there is a sign at the entrance with Adolf Hitler's words, "I want to raise a generation devoid of conscience." Everyone knew what he wanted to have happen. The sign at the door would be a constant reminder to keep this terrible vision alive.

Conversely, the Lord's plan is for us to be guided by conscience, to receive inspiration, insight, and revelation when we ask. In the familiar scripture that led the Prophet Joseph Smith to go to the Lord in prayer, we read, "If any of you lack wisdom, let him ask of God, that giveth to all men liberally, and upbraideth not; and it shall be given him. But let him ask in faith, nothing wavering. For he that wavereth is like a wave of the sea driven with the wind and tossed" (James 1:5-6). The Topical Guide identifies *wisdom* in this setting as guidance, divine learning. When we are guided by the Spirit, we are better prepared to lead, guide, and walk beside, and to share the vision with others.

What happens when a leader fails to share the vision of the work with others who might help? This problem is graphically illustrated in the familiar childhood story of the Little Red Hen. You will remember, she has a great idea. She envisions a day in the future—a day when she will bake bread. This is an ambitious endeavor, given the fact that she has not yet planted the wheat that will one day be used to make the bread. But she is a visionary. She can see the bread, probably even smell it baking in the oven. What a vision for such a little bird! She is not unmindful of the price that will be required: planting, tending, watering, waiting, and ultimately harvesting the wheat, only to be followed by threshing, grinding, and finally using the flour, keeping always in mind the bread—the vision. She evidently feels it worthwhile. You might say she is committed to go all the way.

As the story unfolds, the Little Red Hen wisely approaches others, inviting them to be included, to participate, to work together. But she does not receive a single positive response from any of the farm animals—that is, until the smell of the hot bread is carried on the breeze that sweeps across the barnyard. Suddenly all the inhabitants in this otherwise lazy community are interested and eager to participate. At this moment the Little Red Hen again takes a stand, just as she did following each refusal in times past. "Then I'll do it myself," says the Little Red Hen, and the account confirms that she did.

How might this familiar story have been different if the Little Red Hen had begun her recruiting for help by sharing with the barnyard population her vision? She might have begun by telling of the grand gathering that would be taking place down the road. Everyone would be invited, celebrating those friendships that had been forged while all were laboring together toward a shared goal. She would tell the animals about the good times they would have working together, the new skills they would learn, the new friends they would make. She would invite everyone, including those who were "marginal" barnyard residents, even the rodents. She would tell it with such enthusiasm that when the cow caught the vision and told the pig, who in turn told the turkeys, the whole barnyard would be telling the story loud and clear, and all along the way there would be a constant reminder of the hot bread and honey, a grand gathering celebrating the fellowshipping that had taken place, the unity that had emerged, and the powerful influence for good that the project had become.

When we really share the vision, there may be more volunteers than needed. In the case of the Little Red Hen, the team of happy friends might have made more bread than they could possibly use. They might even have had enough to share with the animals from the neighboring barnyard, and the celebration would have been bigger than she had ever anticipated. Do you think that while the Little Red Hen was eating her bread alone, she might have been thinking, "I worked so hard. I was so dedicated. I never quit. I did everything I knew how. I'm so tired." She might have continued her lament: "I didn't have any help—no support. I had to do it all by myself." If she were given another chance, I think the Little Red Hen would help others see what she saw and feel what she felt for this ambitious project.

KEEPING THE VISION

In all plans and activities, it is important to rehearse over and over what it is we want to have happen in the lives of people. A leader must never show discouragement among those she leads. There will be times of frustration, impatience, and maybe disappointment—but not discouragement, which is a tool of the adversary. It has been my experience that whenever something of great importance arises that could make a significant difference for good in the world, the adversary will marshal all his forces to thwart its progress. Progress is usually stopped when the burden of the work overshadows the purpose, thus causing people to lose the vision. This is followed by a tendency to murmur and complain, and those involved may find themselves like the young woman swimming when the fog moved in. A leader keeps the vision alive.

When the pioneers were bogged down in mud, discouraged by adversity, and might have lost hope because of hardships, the vision of their leader was critical. Consider the vital importance of the vision in the following historic account:

"In the summer of 1862 the foundation of the Salt Lake temple, owing to some defect in its structure, was taken out and relaid. Considering the fact that the foundation was 16 feet deep, and 16 feet broad; and that the building is 186½ feet by 99 feet–this was no small undertaking." Imagine the feelings of the people who had labored under such adverse circumstances. Then think how they caught the vision of their leader as the account continues: "President Young said he expected this temple to stand through the millennium, and the brethren would go in and give the endowments to the people during that time; 'and this,' he added, 'is the reason why I am having the foundation of the temple taken up.' President Young also said on that occasion: '. . . This plan was shown to me in a vision when I first came onto the ground'–meaning the Temple Square where these remarks were made" (B. H. Roberts, *Comprehensive History of the Church*, 6 vols. [Provo, UT: BYU Press, 1965], 5:136).

There are many, perhaps even most, things that we cannot see with our eyes, but the vision of our work is often communicated to us in our mind and heart by the Holy Ghost (see D&C 8:2).

CELEBRATING THE VISION

There will be many occasions for celebrating the realization of the vision. Some accomplishments are of enormous magnitude, whereas others may be only minor, but every step that moves us forward in this great work gives reason for celebration, a celebration filled with gratitude and thanksgiving for all that has been accomplished through the help of the Lord. Daniel H. Wells, an apostle in the early days of the Church, writes of a celebration, the realization of a vision, in these words: "Among all the anniversaries that might be celebrated, that the memory dwells upon, with peculiar feelings of interest, of recollections dire, and deep fraught with every emotion to which the human heart is susceptible, this, the 24th day of July, the anniversary of the arrival of the pioneers in this valley, has been selected as the dawning of a brighter day, as an era in the history of this people upon which turned the axis of their destiny" (in Andrew Jenson, *Journal History of the Church,* July 24, 1851, p. 2). The grand realization of that vision of a Zion to spring up in the Rocky Mountains continues to be celebrated every July 24th even in our day.

Just as the pioneers were seeking to build up Zion, we too in our time are contributing to that same vision. The scale may be smaller, but the vision and the celebration are just as important. Picture, for example, a Primary leader's vision of a group of children all singing together, or nearly so, the song "I'm Trying to Be like Jesus." In the beginning she tells them about the special program they will be participating in, how everyone is needed. She teaches them the words in short phrases and then the meaning. She works to have them follow her hand as she moves high and low in teaching the tune. On the day of the program, she gives the signal to begin as she motions to this little flock to smile. In unison, with a few exceptions, the children's voices touch the hearts of all present as they sing with feeling, "I'm trying to be like Jesus." The program is inspiring but, more important, after the program is over, within the mind and heart of each child are the words that keep that vision alive for years and years to come: "I'm trying to be like Jesus." The Lord said, "Feed my sheep. Feed my lambs." Can one possibly estimate the worth of the contribution made by a Primary leader with vision?

We must understand the value of vision, the importance of getting the vision, the strength and power in sharing the vision, the responsibility of keeping the vision, and the joy in celebrating a realization of the vision. When things go well, leaders with vision give credit to others, celebrating, complimenting, and commending all who have taken part. When things don't go well, effective leaders avoid placing blame. They accept responsibility and learn from every opportunity. Things don't always turn out the way we hope or plan, but the lessons we learn along the way may in the long run prove to be even more valuable than a successful event. We still give thanks for having had a part in the program. Our task may seem small, but the benefits of our labors are eternal in nature. May God help us to catch the vision, to share the vision, and to meet our responsibility in regard to the vision of our work in his kingdom.

CHAPTER THREE

THE FIRE OF COMMITMENT

*O ye that embark in the service of God, see that ye serve
him with all your heart, might, mind and strength, that
ye may stand blameless before God at the last day.*

D & C 4 : 2

One great challenge of leadership is to help those we work
with become totally committed and dependable, able to
follow through and go the extra mile, if needed, to get the job
done. Such commitment is forged in the fire of a burning
desire. A leader fueled with righteous desire and complete
commitment can ignite those around her. When others
become fueled with that same fire, the resources available to a
worthy cause are unlimited, and much is accomplished. In the
absence of desire and commitment there can be frustration,
disappointment, and missed opportunities. Leadership in this
church requires "heart, might, mind and strength" (D&C 4:2),
and we learn from revelation that "if ye have desires to serve
God ye are called to the work" (D&C 4:3).

There may be times when we are called to the work that
our desire needs a little more fuel. It may even need to be
ignited in the first place. Maybe you don't want to be responsible for the tuna-canning project this year; you did it last year
and the smell has never left you. Maybe you aren't ready to
accept the calling as activities specialist in the ward. Maybe you
don't want to lie in a sleeping bag at girls camp one more year.
Whatever the calling, in the absence of desire there can be
little, if any, sustained commitment. Desire precedes commitment. It sometimes begins only as a tiny seed. If necessary, let
it begin there. If it is a good seed, it will grow (see Alma 32).

ENTHUSIASM AND KNOWLEDGE

Desire and commitment manifest themselves in enthusiasm. Although you may feel that you lack the confidence and experience of a more seasoned leader, enthusiasm will open doors that might otherwise seem impossible to budge. I learned this years ago when I was employed by the Mountain States Telephone Company. One day the manager, Mr. Wallace, called me into his office to advise me that I had been selected to a supervisory position in the business office of the company. I was surprised. I immediately began explaining to him that I was relatively new and that there were others who had much more experience and knowledge and capability than I. He did not hesitate to agree, explaining that he was very much aware of my limitations but adding, "What you lack in experience, you make up for with your enthusiasm, and you will learn the rest." I was complimented by his trust. Yes, I could be enthusiastic, but I soon learned that that was not enough—not nearly enough.

In the article "Zeal without Knowledge," by Hugh Nibley, we see the essential nature of both characteristics. *Zeal* is defined in the dictionary as "industry, enthusiasm, animation, vigor, earnestness, passion, devotion." Brother Nibley explains: "Zeal is the engine that drives the whole vehicle: without it we would get nowhere. But without clutch, throttle, brakes, and a steering wheel, our mighty engine becomes an instrument of destruction, and the more powerful the motor, the more disastrous the inevitable crack-up if the proper knowledge is lacking" (*Approaching Zion* [Salt Lake City: Deseret Book and F.A.R.M.S., 1989], p. 69).

Zeal and enthusiasm are powerful tools when used in a timely manner. The story is told of a minister who supposedly invited his congregation to stand and recite in unison the 23rd Psalm, and then requested that the lady in the audience who always arrived at the "green pastures" before the rest, "Please wait there for the others to catch up." A leader must lead out, but timing and order and a sensitivity to those whom we are to lead, guide, and walk beside are also important.

Enthusiasm, desire, and commitment are essential. They are the fuel that fires the engine. We cannot succeed without them. However, this power can evaporate like dew in the morning sun unless it is captured and sustained by a leader who has the vision and knowledge, understands the purpose, and can share it with others.

Elder Sterling W. Sill explained: "The nearest word to 'fire' in meaning and function is probably 'enthusiasm,' which is a kind of fire in the soul, producing soul power. The word 'enthusiasm' came from the Greek words 'en' and 'theos' which means 'God in us' or 'divine inspiration.' . . .

"There are not many fire kindlers, not many fire carriers, not many who bring us sparks from the divine. . . . Intelligent enthusiasm probably makes a greater contribution to success than any other single trait" (*Leadership*, 3 vols. [Salt Lake City: Bookcraft, 1958], 1:100-101). When the Spirit leaves the body, the body gets cold. This is also what happens when desire and commitment leave leadership.

OUR OWN COMMITMENT

Consider conducting a private interview with yourself by asking: What is my level of commitment—my heart's desire—relating to my leadership responsibilities? Am I halfhearted or wholehearted? Do I want all of the blessings or part of them? Do I need a heart transplant—a change of heart—before I'm ready to lead, guide, and walk beside others? Can the fire I carry, like sparks from the divine, help others as they grow in leadership skills and attributes?

A familiar hymn that expresses an attitude of commitment, sung often at missionary farewells, applies equally well to our call as leaders in the Church wherever we serve:

> It may not be on the mountain height
> Or over the stormy sea,

It may not be at the battle's front
My Lord will have need of me.
But if, by a still, small voice he calls
To paths that I do not know,
I'll answer, dear Lord, with my hand in thine:
I'll go where you want me to go.

Perhaps today there are loving words
Which Jesus would have me speak;
There may be now in the paths of sin
Some wand'rer whom I should seek.
O Savior, if thou wilt be my guide,
Tho dark and rugged the way,
My voice shall echo the message sweet:
I'll say what you want me to say.

There's surely somewhere a lowly place
In earth's harvest fields so wide
Where I may labor through life's short day
For Jesus, the Crucified.
So trusting my all to thy tender care,
And knowing thou lovest me,
I'll do thy will with a heart sincere:
I'll be what you want me to be.

(Hymns, no. 270)

Elder John A. Widtsoe explained: "In our preexistent state, in the day of the great council, we made a certain agreement with the Almighty. The Lord proposed a plan, conceived by him. We accepted it. . . . We agreed, right then and there, to be not only saviors for ourselves but measurably, saviors for the whole human family. We went into a partnership with the Lord" (*Utah Genealogical and Historical Magazine,* October 1934, p. 189). Our covenants, properly understood, form the foundation for our commitment. Nephi's example provides a model for us: "I will go and do the things which the Lord hath commanded, for I know that the Lord giveth no commandments unto the children of men, save he shall prepare a way for them that they may accomplish the thing which he commandeth them" (1 Nephi 3:7).

When we stand undecided and uncommitted, our vulnerability to every wind that blows becomes life-threatening. Uncertainty, the thief of time and commitment, breeds vacillation and confusion.

Commitment requires a level of self-mastery, self-discipline, the ability to make ourselves do what we ought to do until it becomes what we want to do. It has been said, "Where there is no discipline, Christ has no disciples." President Spencer W. Kimball will long be remembered for his favorite saying: "Do it!"

A LEADER'S CHALLENGE

Leaders have the constant challenge to keep alive the commitment to the work and to fuel that fire in others. Whether our leadership responsibilities are in Primary, Young Women, Sunday School, or Relief Society, whether we are working to reach the less active, touch the nonmember, or maintain the commitment of members, there are some principles that apply. These principles are well known to most missionaries and are often referred to as the commitment pattern. I believe it is an excellent pattern for leadership.

1. Build a relationship of trust, love, and respect.
2. Help people feel the Spirit.
3. Bear testimony and invite participation.
4. Resolve any concerns that may be felt by asking questions that invite understanding.
5. Help people recognize that it is the Spirit they are feeling.
6. Seek commitment by identifying what is to be done and asking in a forthright way, "Will you?"

This commitment pattern applies to much more than missionary work. For example, once when I was in Australia speaking to a group of adult leaders, I asked a young woman in the audience who had just turned twelve to come forward and tell us of a recent activity her class had participated in. She was a bit hesitant at first, but then told of how her class had gone to her teacher's home and made cookies—a good time to build relationships of trust, unless the leader is more focused on the cookies than the opportunity to talk and listen to the girls. I asked this young woman what they did with the cookies (after they ate a few, of course). She told me they went as a group to an old folks home to share the cookies (putting them in a position to feel the Spirit and inviting their participation). I asked her how she felt about that experience, hoping to help her feel and recognize the Spirit. She said at first it was scary. I asked a follow-up question, "And then what happened?" This young woman explained that she had given her cookies to a lady. I waited for her further response. She continued, "She patted my hand and had tears in her eyes." Then another question: "How did you feel?" Her voice softened. She looked not at the audience as before, but at me, with a tender expression, as if she were making a discovery for the first time about how she had felt. Putting her hand over her heart, she said, "I felt warm right here." I asked, "Do you know what that feeling is?" She shook her head, indicating she didn't know. I bore testimony to her that the feeling was the Spirit, that it was a testimony of her service. Her eyes lit up and she exclaimed excitedly, "Really? A testimony? I didn't know I had one." She put her hand back over her heart as though to rekindle that feeling.

Was making cookies the purpose the leader had in mind? I think not. The activity was only a means to the end. But unless a leader follows up on the trust-building activity by asking find-out questions, and helps her followers recognize and feel the Spirit, the activity may end up being just that—an activity, and a lost opportunity. When people can feel the Spirit about the work to be done and gain a testimony of what can happen in the lives of others as a result of their service, they will feel a natural desire to be involved. When a leader focuses on programs rather than people, it may be more difficult to rally a team of committed participants. But put someone's life on the line, and volunteers come out of the woodwork, so to speak, to rescue those in need—even if they are strangers.

I've come to believe that even the slightest effort that strengthens another's commitment to live the gospel is a form of rescue. At girls camp one year, the young women were invited to go out in nature alone and kneel down in prayer before returning home. Following the camping experience, in the next fast and testimony meeting in her ward, one young woman stood and testified, "I went out by myself. I knelt down. I didn't know what to say, so I just said, 'Heavenly Father, do you know I am here?'" She said she waited. She could hear the wind in the trees. She opened her eyes and could see the sun filtering through the leaves. Pausing in her description, she then testified, "I just felt warm all over from the top of my head to the bottom of my feet. You may not think it was anything, but I knew He knew I was there." Is one such testimony reward enough for a leader going to girls camp? How many times would someone be willing to participate with that kind of outcome at stake? Is that enough of a reason to be committed to the work?

When people see and feel what can happen as a result of their service in the lives of others, they become committed, fueled with the fire of desire, compelled with a fervor for the work of saving souls. When we are truly committed to reach others through activities that are planned with that purpose, our labors become a sacred mission on the Lord's errand, and the commitment pattern becomes a lasting commitment for all our lives.

PART TWO

LEADERSHIP

SKILLS

CHAPTER FOUR

PRINCIPLES AND PRACTICES

For if the trumpet give an uncertain sound,
who shall prepare himself to the battle?

1 CORINTHIANS 14:8

John Masefield, who went to sea when he was a boy and later became poet laureate, wrote in one of his poems: "All I ask is a tall ship and a star to steer her by." Principles are the stars we steer by, fixed markers used to chart our course on our eternal journey.

In the little booklet *For the Strength of Youth,* the First Presidency places some of these eternal principles in their proper perspective for youth and for all of us:

"God loves you as he loves each and every one of his children. His desire, purpose, and glory is to have you return to him pure and undefiled, having proven yourselves worthy of an eternity of joy in his presence.

"Your Father in Heaven is mindful of you. He has given you commandments to guide you, to discipline you. He has also given you your agency—freedom of choice—'to see if [you] will do all things whatsoever [He] shall command' (Abraham 3:25). Freedom of choice is a God-given, eternal principle that carries with it moral responsibilities for the choices made. . . . We bear witness of the truth of these principles" (*For the Strength of Youth* [Salt Lake City: The Church of Jesus Christ of Latter-day Saints, 1990], pp. 3–4).

When we teach correct principles, without compromise, with clarity and example, we empower others to govern their own lives and make decisions in harmony with these principles. As always, the Savior is our example in teaching and

43

living correct principles. President Spencer W. Kimball said of him:

"Jesus knew who he was and why he was here on this planet. That meant he could lead from strength rather than from uncertainty or weakness.

"Jesus operated from a base of fixed principles or truths rather than making up the rules as he went along. Thus, his leadership style was not only correct, but also constant. So many secular leaders today are like chameleons; they change their hues and views to fit the situation—which only tends to confuse associates and followers who cannot be certain what course is being pursued. Those who cling to power at the expense of principle often end up doing almost anything to perpetuate their power" (*Ensign,* August 1979, p. 5).

As I have considered the importance of principles, I have been reminded of my high school graduation years ago. The commencement speaker, Elder Oscar A. Kirkham, spoke to the graduates of the need to: (1) Build a seaworthy ship, (2) Be a loyal shipmate, and (3) Sail a true course. Guiding principles and laws that remain fixed, steady, and dependable are essential to building character (a seaworthy ship), developing loyalty, and sailing a true course.

BUILD A SEAWORTHY SHIP

Principles can be likened to the framework for the ship which everything rests upon. In The Church of Jesus Christ of Latter-day Saints we have stable, anchored, unchanging principles that are identified in the fourth Article of Faith: "We believe that the first principles and ordinances of the gospel are: first, Faith in the Lord Jesus Christ; second, Repentance; third, Baptism by immersion for the remission of sins; fourth, Laying on of hands for the gift of the Holy Ghost." These true, eternal principles must stand unchanged when our vessel is being prepared for stormy seas. We will have a seaworthy ship that can endure through any storms: temptations, despondency, discouragement and rejection, chastisement or any other storms that may rage.

Helaman explained to his sons: "When the devil shall send forth his mighty winds, yea, his shafts in the whirlwind, yea, when all his hail and his mighty storm shall beat upon you, it shall have no power over you to drag you down to the gulf of misery and endless wo, because of the rock upon which ye are built, which is a sure foundation, a foundation whereon if men build they cannot fall" (Helaman 5:12).

Toni Morrison, an award-winning novelist, writes that from time to time during her childhood, her father would tell her matter-of-factly, "Today I welded the straightest seam on any ship about to sail on any sea, anywhere. Before a slab of metal was welded over it I signed my name on the seam." Each time, Toni reminded him that no one would ever see his signature. Her father answered, "But I saw it."

If we will adhere to true principles as steadfastly as that shipbuilder, regardless of who notices or cares, we too will build a seaworthy ship.

BE A LOYAL SHIPMATE

Holding to principles without compromise, we become trustworthy. We stay on board and never abandon ship, regardless of the pressure or the temptations. This kind of loyalty is graphically illustrated in the movie *Chariots of Fire,* the award-winning story of a Scottish missionary and a Jewish Cambridge student whose principles are clarified against the backdrop of the 1924 Olympic games. Eric, the Scottish athlete, refuses to compromise his principles by running on the Sabbath. He advises: "Don't compromise. Compromise is the language of the devil. Run in God's name and let the world stand back and wonder."

He continues: "Everyone runs in his own way. So where does the fire come from to see the race to its end? It comes from within. Jesus said, 'Behold, the kingdom of God is within you, and if with all your heart you truly seek me, you shall surely find me.' If you commit yourself to the love of Christ . . . that is how you run a straight race."

When we train ourselves to be guided by personal values in harmony with eternal principles, we look beyond the race, beyond the moment. We join with those spoken of by Isaiah: "But they that wait upon the Lord shall renew their strength; they shall mount up with wings as eagles; they shall run, and not be weary; and they shall walk, and not faint" (Isaiah 40:31).

Even in the worst of times, the best is available to anyone who remains loyal to eternal and unchanging principles. President Gordon B. Hinckley quotes John Engler, governor of Michigan, as saying: "The wisdom of the ages reveals that our moral compass cannot ultimately come from Lansing or from any other state capital, any more than it can come from the nation's capital, or Hollywood, or the United Nations, or some abstract liberal conception of the 'Village.' It comes from deep within us—it comes from our character, which is forged in our families and our faith and tempered in the arena of decision making and action" (As quoted in *Teachings of Gordon B. Hinckley* [Salt Lake City: Deseret Book, 1997], p. 384).

SAIL A TRUE COURSE

As leaders in the Church, we are given an infallible guide when we are in tune with the Spirit. We have the power of discernment through the gift of the Holy Ghost.

Years ago, on the ditchbanks in southern Alberta, my father taught me about the importance of listening for the inner bell. As usual, his lesson began with a story:

"There was an old and very large inch cape rock," he said. "It got its name from being located just one inch below the water's surface where it couldn't be seen. And it lay dangerously in the path of the mariners returning from sea. Many seamen had lost their ships and their lives because of the rock, especially in times of storm." I now was drawn into the story, but I had yet to learn what this had to do with a bell.

Dad continued, "There was an Abbott in the small seashore

town of Aberbrothok who devised a solution to this life-threatening hazard. With great care and in the face of considerable danger, the Abbott fastened a buoy with a large bell on it to the inch cape rock. From then on the bell rang continuously and faithfully with the motion of the waves of the sea, and mariners would bless the name of the Abbott who had placed it there."

Now the plot thickened. One villager, Ralph the Rover, was a bit of a pirate who disliked the Abbott, and disliked even more the praises the Abbott received from the mariners whose lives his bell spared. So one day Ralph the Rover cut the bell from the inch cape rock. Here Dad would burst into rhyme:

> *Down sank the bell with a gurgling sound;*
> *The bubbles rose, and burst around.*
> *Quoth Sir Ralph, "The next who comes to the Rock*
> *Won't bless the Abbott of Aberbrothok."*
>
> *Sir Ralph, the Rover, sailed away,*
> *He scoured the seas for many a day.*

More narrative followed, leading to Ralph's nighttime return. The sea was high and he had thought the moon would be up, but it was not. In the darkness he said, with great anxiety (but only to himself), "I wish I could hear the bell of the inch cape rock."

Then the verse:

> *Sir Ralph, the Rover, tore his hair;*
> *He cursed himself in his despair.*
> *The waves rush in on every side;*
> *The ship is sinking beneath the tide.*
>
> (Robert Southey, "The Inch Cape Rock")

I have thought often of the inner bell with its constant peal and have felt myself strain a little that I might hear it more clearly as I face the storms of life. How foolish we would be to cut away that bell, cut ourselves off from eternal principles, in a moment of weakness or spite.

When we are riveted to eternal principles, we can point the way and help others maneuver safely through stormy seas. Of our responsibility as leaders to clarify and defend true principles, President Kimball wrote: "We continue to warn the people and plead with them, for we are watchmen upon the towers, and in our hands we have a trumpet which we must blow loudly and sound the alarm. . . . It would be a poor lighthouse that gave off a different signal to guide every ship entering a harbor" (*The Teachings of Spencer W. Kimball* [Salt Lake City: Bookcraft, 1982], p. 484).

Leaders must be strong, consistent, and stable under pressure. People, especially youth, find security in leaders who stand by correct principles, uphold them, and teach them by example. Nephi and Lehi described the word of God as an iron rod. It is fixed and undeviating. When an individual chooses to let go of that rod and wanders from the course for a time, either deliberately or unintentionally, still in his or her mind is the knowledge of where the rod is and what would be required to correct the course. If principles are not taught with clarity, and there is no iron rod in place, there is no marker to help us make those course corrections.

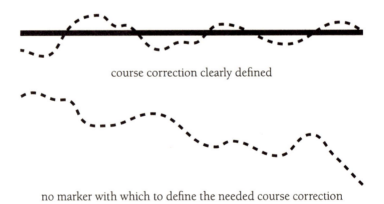

course correction clearly defined

no marker with which to define the needed course correction

While serving as general Young Women president, I received many letters from youth asking for clarification of

48

principles. One example begins with large letters in bold print across the top, "Urgent, Answer Fast!"

"Dear Sister Kapp,

"I would like to ask you a question concerning the appropriate dance style at the church dances. In our stake, the stake Young Women's president has allowed the youth to bear hug on the slow dances. I don't feel this is the proper way to dance. Can you please tell us if this is the right way to dance?"

Another young woman writes:

"I am thirteen years old, almost fourteen. My birthday is December 5th. I am writing you this letter concerning being able to go to dances at my school. I would have my parents or one of my friends' parents take me and pick me up after the dance. I would not have a date, I would dance with a whole bunch of different boys. I know this sounds like a lame excuse, but all my friends' parents don't care if they go and they are also Mormons."

Is it possible that we as leaders, including parents, would contribute to uncertainty in teaching principles? I can't help but contrast those examples with an experience from my own early teenage years. I was almost sixteen, and the annual ward dance was coming up. I pleaded to go, offering all sorts of persuasive arguments and possible compromises. After a lengthy discussion, my mother changed the focus. "It is not the dance," she explained. "The dance is not the issue. It is the principle." That didn't make sense to me at the time, but she persisted. "It is the principle, the principle of obedience. That is the basis upon which we must make this decision." The lesson I learned from staying home was of eternal worth.

PRINCIPLES VERSUS PRACTICES

Sometimes confusion arises because people fail to differentiate between principles and practices. Principles are unchanging. Practices may change to accommodate various circumstances. For example, at one time there was a practice that women should not wear pants in the chapel. Letters came inquiring about this practice. Women in Alaska dressed for survival in cold weather were coming to the church carrying their dresses and changing in the restroom or staying in the foyer. Other letters came from Asian Saints whose culture accepted a dress style including pants, even for formal occasions. In the little booklet *For the Strength of Youth,* we read a clear statement of principle that accommodates the various practices: "Servants of God have always counseled his children to dress modestly to show respect for him and for themselves. . . . Avoid tight fitting or revealing clothes and extremes in clothing and appearance . . . dressing appropriately for Church meetings and activities" (*For the Strength of Youth,* p. 8). The principle, respect for God and yourself, can be honored in different ways when circumstances dictate.

I have been around long enough to remember when all matters pertaining to the women's organizations of the Church were funneled through the ward and stake auxiliary leaders to the auxiliary leaders at Church headquarters. From Salt Lake we received bulletins and specific direction on what to do and when. People came to the great MIA June conference from far and wide. (It doesn't seem so far and wide now, considering how the Church is expanding and extending throughout the nations of the world today.) There we received all we needed to know to run the programs, including the scripts and sometimes even the props.

When those things ended, it was a difficult time of transition for some. The communication line was changed. In order to accommodate the growth of the Church, the responsibility for making decisions had to be carried by the local leaders, within established principles and guidelines. Auxiliary leaders on the ward and stake level would now counsel with their local priesthood leaders. Leaders, men and women, would be prepared to receive direction for their stewardship locally and seek inspiration individually. As the Church continues to grow, practices must be examined and changed if necessary, but eternal principles will never be outdated.

In our desire to be loyal shipmates and sail a true course, we may be unsettled and confused, and may even compromise if we look at the issue without considering the principle. Principles are commandments or laws that the Lord has provided to serve as a sure compass and pilot us through stormy seas until we arrive safely home.

When leaders learn, teach, and practice correct principles, they become pilots, guides to those they lead until they reach the shore. President J. Reuben Clark Jr., speaking to those who would lead and teach, said: "The mere possession of a testimony is not enough. You must have besides this, one of the rarest and most precious of all the many elements of human character—moral courage. For in the absence of moral courage to declare your testimony, it will reach the students only after such dilution as will make it difficult if not impossible for them to detect it; and the spiritual and psychological effect of a weak and vacillating testimony may well be actually harmful instead of helpful" ("The Charted Course of the Church in Education," as quoted in Boyd K. Packer, *Teach Ye Diligently* [Salt Lake City: Deseret Book, 1975], pp. 314-15).

Elder Bruce R. McConkie reminds us of the ever-increasing responsibility leaders today share in clarifying principles. He writes: "I think the world is going to get worse, and the faithful portion of the Church, at least, is going to get better. The day is coming, more than ever has been the case in the past, when we will be under the obligation of making a choice, of standing up for the Church, of adhering to its precepts and teachings and principles, of taking the counsel that comes from the apostles and prophets whom God has placed to teach the doctrine and bear witness to the world. The day is coming when this will be more necessary" (*Ensign,* November 1974, p. 35).

In a spirit of unity and commitment, working together we can withstand the increasing opposition and be a light on a hill. Although principles, like the North Star, are fixed and remain constant, practices, traditions, and habits can and sometimes must change if the resources available within the Church are to be maximized for the benefit of individuals and families. Our world is changing. May we know when to be flexible and when to remain firm as we lead the way for others.

CHAPTER FIVE

PLANNING AND GOALS

*I will go and do the things which the Lord hath
commanded, for I know that the Lord giveth no
commandments unto the children of men, save he shall
prepare a way for them that they may accomplish
the thing which he commandeth them.*

1 NEPHI 3:7

I have always been intrigued by the conversation between the Cheshire cat and Alice in the classic novel *Alice in Wonderland* by Lewis Carroll. Alice began with a question: "Will you please tell me which way I ought to walk from here?"

The cat answered: "That depends a good deal on where you want to get to."

"I don't much care where," Alice replied.

"Then it doesn't matter which way you walk."

"Just so I get somewhere," she hastily added.

"Oh, you are sure to do that, if only you walk far enough," was the cat's reply.

Alice's problem is linked to a dilemma most leaders face at some point: lack of planning. If we want to go in the right direction, we need to have a clearly defined goal and a plan to meet that goal. "Make no small plans; they have no magic to stir men's souls," is the counsel of President Spencer W. Kimball. Emily Dickinson penned these lines:

> We never know how high we are
> Till we are called to rise
> And then, if we are true to plan
> Our statures touch the skies.

Planning in advance and with a purpose is essential to effective leadership. Planning becomes natural once we understand the reason for it. A well-developed plan can be exciting because it allows us to live in anticipation of accomplishing something we can see in our minds. Planning identifies the steps necessary to reach a goal. The key to being effective is planning with a purpose. We simply ask the question, "What do we as an organization, a group, or an individual want to have happen?" Once that goal is clearly understood, effective planning can begin.

Time spent in effective planning with a purpose will greatly reduce the time required to execute the plan. It will also increase the probability of accomplishing the desired outcome. In the absence of such planning, all the effort may be for naught.

Attending a youth conference that concluded with a dance, I had a brief conversation with two young women who were sitting on the floor in the corner of the rest room talking to each other. They were dressed appropriately for the dance, so I couldn't resist inquiring as to why they weren't participating in it. "We like it better here," they said. "The music is so loud we can't hear each other, and we want to talk. It is quieter in here." There was no question about that.

I took occasion to ask one of the leaders in a gentle way about the plans for the dance. He explained with some enthusiasm that the youth had come from a long distance, and many of them were the only Church members in their schools. This dance provided a wonderful opportunity for them to get together and become acquainted. "You know there is strength in numbers," he said.

One might ask in this situation: If the music is so loud that the youth can't hear each other, and the lights are so low that they can't see each other, is there any way that the purpose for having the dance—to become acquainted with each other—can be realized? The purpose for the dance was clear and good, but the plan did not serve the purpose. Following the steps in planning with a purpose can greatly reduce the possibility of missed opportunity.

GOAL SETTING

Benjamin Franklin reportedly said, "Living without a goal is like shooting without a target." Goals are simply specific targets, desired outcomes that individuals or organizations strive to accomplish in a specific period of time. Goals help leaders become results oriented instead of task oriented.

A goal is an anticipated event. With goals, we can bring the future into the present and begin working toward it immediately. We begin to live in anticipation, looking forward to what will be. Clearly defined goals give us a reason for doing some things and laying aside others, a reason for sustained effort and motivation. Goal setting not only helps clarify what we will do but also releases us from the myriad of things we choose not to do. Until we make the decision about what we will do, we are crippled by thoughts of all the things we should or would do if time were of no essence. But it is!

Having goals provides a basis for decision making. In each case we can appeal to the goals we have set as a court in which to evaluate the effectiveness of our actions and activities. As leaders we must ask: "Will this plan, this activity, this party, this event lead toward or away from our purpose?"

The first step in identifying a goal is to take a look at things as they are: the strengths of the organization, the areas needing improvement, and the specific needs of individuals and families. This can be done individually, as a presidency, or as a board, but eventually everyone needs to be informed and involved. Counseling together provides information and inspiration.

From a group effort there will come many worthy goals. The next step is to prioritize those goals in order of importance. This gives order and focus to those things that matter most and to what it is you want to have happen.

It has been said that "goals that are not written are merely wishes." The leader of an organization needs written goals that can be circulated freely, referred to frequently, and evaluated regularly. Shared goals become the foundation of a united effort focused on a desired outcome.

Goals are most effective when they are specific and measurable and, when appropriate, have a date for completion. An example of such a goal would be the one given by the Relief Society president in my ward: "Every sister will receive the help she needs to identify at least one name from her family history and be prepared to take it to the temple by September 1998." Notice that the goal is specific, measurable, and has a time for completion. A long-term goal like this one might be strengthened by being broken down into shorter intervals. With interim target dates at regular intervals, motivation for reaching the goal is increased.

In the Young Women organization, for example, the goal is to have every young woman prepare to make and keep sacred covenants and receive the ordinances of the temple. That is a long-range goal for a twelve-year-old. However, there are many interim goals leading to that desired outcome. A Beehive is to become a young woman of truth, with specific objectives that qualify her for that accomplishment. The same is true for a Mia Maid, a young woman of promise, and a Laurel, a young woman of faith. A young woman learning to set and reach goals will ultimately be prepared to make and keep covenants, the desired long-range outcome.

Consider this goal of the Primary: Every girl and boy will have memorized the thirteen Articles of Faith and be prepared to recite them by the time he or she graduates from Primary. This is another example of a specific goal that is measurable and has a completion date. This ultimate goal is broken down into thirteen smaller goals so that acknowledgment for accomplishment can be given at regular intervals—a good practice in any goal-setting activity.

PLANNING WITH A PURPOSE

After goals are clearly and specifically identified, it is then time to make plans for how to accomplish what it is you want to have happen. This step is called planning with a purpose. Recall a time when you as a leader had a specific purpose for an activity clearly in mind. In evaluating after the event, when you realized that you had accomplished the goal, didn't you feel exhilarated, enthused, rewarded, and repaid many times for your effort? You knew where you were headed. You could measure your progress along the way, and you knew when you had arrived.

Now, try to recall a time when you worked hard and spent a lot of time and effort on an activity that was just that: an activity, without any real purpose other than to keep a group busily involved in something. Did you feel a sense of accomplishment, or were you just tired and glad to get it over with? If you didn't know where you were trying to go, how would you know if you got there? As a counselor in a Relief Society presidency explained to me: "Leadership without planning brings one crisis after another in constant regularity, or it brings nothing at all."

The following format can be helpful when followed in proper sequence:

Planning with a Purpose

Goal	Plans	Action/Event	Evaluation

Step 1. Determine the specific goal by deciding what it is you want to have happen. Goals and plans are inextricably linked. Both are needed if you are going to achieve what you

are capable of. Under the heading "Goal," write as specifically and succinctly as possible what you want to have happen.

Step 2. Make a plan that is thoughtfully designed to accomplish the goal. This is done by examining where you are (current status) and what needs to be done to get you where you want to be (desired outcome). The purpose of a plan is to remove any obstacle and provide the needed resources to accomplish the goal.

In the initial stages of developing a plan, taking an opportunity for brainstorming can be helpful. This provides for many ideas and possibilities and helps generate enthusiasm and support for the final plan among those involved in the process.

Brainstorming is an unstructured discussion in which all ideas related to the goal are worthy of consideration. Everyone's contribution is of equal importance. The leader's comments are not to be valued more than those of any other participant at this point. In fact, it is a good idea for the leader to withhold comments or suggestions initially to encourage the free flow of ideas from others. All members of the group exchange ideas. It is important to have a recorder to capture the ideas as they flow. No evaluation of the ideas takes place at this stage.

After this general discussion with a reasonable time limit, it is time to bring a more formal structure to the meeting. When the ideas have been discussed, the leader then takes her place as the leader. The planning continues as she processes the information, responds to questions and comments, makes a proposal, and seeks support for the plan.

Step 3. Act on the plan. Action is the key to any plan. Establishing goals and making plans for achieving them can be meaningful only if specific assignments are made, identifying who will do what, and when. A leader will emphasize the importance of sticking to the plan. As the saying goes, "Plan your work and work your plan."

Step 4. Follow up and report back. At the time an assignment is given, it should be recorded with specific dates for following up and reporting back. A major weakness in most leadership and planning comes from failure to follow up and get regular reports on progress being made. Following up and reporting back provides an opportunity to make any necessary adjustments, accommodate unexpected circumstances, provide commendation and encouragement, and feel confident that the plan is being implemented in accordance with the purpose. This step will dramatically increase the probability for success. A leader should be kept informed and thus avoid, where possible, any unwelcome surprises.

Step 5. Evaluate. Learn from your experience. Where possible, it is good to include all those involved in the planning in an evaluation meeting following the implementation of the plan. Regardless of the outcome, the leader should acknowledge the work done, give commendation where appropriate, and express appreciation. Begin by referring back to the plan and asking, "Did our planning accomplish the purpose?" Opportunities should be provided for a brief report from those involved. It is desirable to focus first on what went well and why. Then it is very important to discuss what might have been done to improve the plan and how it might have been carried out. Some of the best leadership training takes place in the evaluation meeting following the event. This is especially true with young or inexperienced leaders.

Leadership principles learned in one calling or assignment can be applied in many other assignments that are sure to come. Often one of the most important benefits that can come from an assignment is the leadership experience that is gained and principles of leadership that are taught. A record of the evaluation meeting can be invaluable for future planning.

Planning with a purpose can be practiced in the home with all members of the family. I shall never forget the first year we as a family decided to use the idea of planning with a purpose for our Christmas activities. We gathered children and adults, cousins, aunts, uncles, brothers, and sisters together. I asked the question, "What do we want to have happen this year when we are all together for Christmas?" The answer seemed a little self-evident, but I waited and eventually the list began: Have presents, act out the Nativity, eat turkey, read the Bible, sing songs. I stopped the comments and said, "Wonderful. That is what we are going to *do*. But what do we want to have *happen?*" There was a sense of wonderment. We had managed very well without this kind of deliberation in the past. Why this approach? was the thoughtful expression on some faces. One of the youth in the group, a budding young leader, said, "You mean like an agenda?" And then with some concern in her voice, she added, "For Christmas?"

"No, not an agenda for Christmas," I assured her. "But what do we want to feel, to learn, to know, or to remember that will be important after the turkey is gone and the gifts are all forgotten?" This invited a different conversation and provided a wonderful list of things we as a family had never considered before. One of the young children said, "I'd like to know what Christmas was like when Grandpa and Grandma were alive." A comment from another member, "I think it would be fun if our family could start a new tradition, just for our family." And from another came the suggestion, "How could we feel more grateful for all we have and thoughtful of those who are less fortunate?" The ideas continued to flow.

We began to plan our Christmas that year with a purpose, and that has affected all the subsequent Christmases in a significant way. Specific assignments were made and everyone had a part. The young and less experienced were assisted by those who were prepared to help. In an attempt to experience Christmas like Grandpa and Grandma, we bought a small Christmas tree and on Christmas Eve gathered together to decorate the little tree with long, thin, silver icicles, just like Grandpa and Grandma had. It was a wonderful experience until one of the children, impatient with putting the icicles on one by one, took a handful and tossed them on the tree.

Next we all went to the cemetery with our little tree and placed it beside Grandpa and Grandma's grave. We stood in a circle and talked about the meaning of Christmas. The light breeze blew the icicles and the evening sun cast a glow on the little tree, giving it the appearance of being alive. We talked about the meaning of Christmas, that because of Jesus we can one day all be together again as a family.

The idea of a new family tradition began by going down to the bridge where Grandpa used to walk. We all stood close together and managed to tie a big red ribbon around our family as a symbol of our being tied together forever. Our desire to help those less fortunate led us to make a small donation in the name of each of the children to help buy a water buffalo for a family in Africa.

Each plan was carried out with a purpose. And after Christmas, when we talked about what we liked best, it was decided by one and all that in the future we would use planning with a purpose for every Christmas. What we wanted to have happen, happened, and much, much more.

Whether at home, in the Church, or in other leadership situations, when meaningful goals are identified and plans are made with a purpose in mind, wonderful things can happen.

CHAPTER SIX

MEETINGS

Organize yourselves; prepare every needful thing;
and establish a house, even a house of prayer, a house of
fasting, a house of faith, a house of learning,
a house of glory, a house of order, a house of God.

D&C 88:119

It is a weighty responsibility to call people together for a meeting. One brother, giving the invocation in a stake leadership meeting where many had gathered, prayed that "the benefits from this meeting will prove to be more important than what we might otherwise be doing." That thought-provoking and worthy prayer emphasizes the responsibility of those who plan and conduct meetings and those who attend.

At the close of a two-hour leadership training meeting for which I had some responsibility and obvious concern, the Regional Representative in attendance stood to make a few closing remarks. In a warm and inviting manner, he stated, "It takes a good meeting to be better than no meeting at all," then added with a word of appreciation, "and this was a good meeting."

Question: What makes a good meeting?
Answer: If it accomplishes the purpose
for which it was called.

Question: What should be the purpose?
Answer: It all depends on the need.

For example, we might apply this more specifically to the question: What makes a good family home evening? If it is to be a planning meeting for a family vacation, the purpose would be quite different from that of a family home evening designed to prepare an eight-year-old family member for baptism.

The purpose of a meeting will vary depending on the organization, the area of responsibility, and the needs of the individuals involved. But common to every meeting in the Church is the focus that must consume all our efforts as leaders. President Boyd K. Packer has spoken of this overriding responsibility: "We urge you now to concentrate on the mission of the Church rather than to merely manage organizations and programs. . . . You may wonder how to proceed to implement the mission of the Church in the lives of your members. Where should you focus your attention and energy? . . . We are to bring to pass the immortality and eternal life of man by concentrating on *ordinances* and on the *covenants* associated with them. . . . If we will set . . . our mind to the words *ordinance* and *covenant,* and then look up, light will come through. Then you will know how to fix your position and plot your course. . . . A good and useful and true test of every major decision made by a leader in the Church is whether a given course leads toward or away from the making and keeping of covenants. . . . We would do well to see that in administering the organizations of the Church, *all roads lead to the temple.* For it is there that we are prepared in all things to qualify us to enter the presence of the Lord" (Address at Regional Representatives seminar, April 3, 1987; emphasis added. As quoted in M. Russell Ballard, *Counseling with Our Councils* [Salt Lake City: Deseret Book, 1997], p. 124).

This is the ultimate goal for all of our labors. The question, "What do we want to have happen?" remains the same. But each organization, according to the different needs of the individuals in that organization, will have a different "how" this is to be accomplished.

Meetings are held for the purpose of communicating and acting on information that will make a difference in people's lives. Meetings held within the organization of the Church begin with the family home evening and extend beyond the family (for the purpose of strengthening the individual and the family) to include priesthood meetings, auxiliary meetings, planning meetings, committee meetings, leadership meetings, evaluation meetings, council meetings, welfare meetings, bishop's youth committee meetings, and many, many more. These meetings are conducted by people of all ages and experience (and inexperience), but a few guiding principles can help in conducting effective meetings on any level.

1. It is usually more effective when meetings can be planned for a regular time and place.

2. Use a written agenda. An agenda is simply a written plan or outline prepared in advance of the meeting. The leader conducting the meeting uses it to provide focus and order to the items for presentation, discussion, or action. Without a well-planned agenda and a time frame to work within, the focus and purpose for the meeting can be lost and time wasted.

3. Start and end on time. This is sometimes difficult, but it helps keep the focus on the meeting and increases the need to be well prepared.

4. Begin and end with prayer, and usually include a scripture or spiritual thought.

5. Focus on one or more aspects of the mission of the Church: proclaiming the gospel (missionary work), perfecting the Saints (preparing for and participating in ordinances and covenants), and redeeming the dead (family history and temple work). It should be noted that in each case attention should focus first on the needs of individuals and then on programs designed to help meet those needs.

6. All activities should be planned with a purpose.

7. When making assignments, include dates for following up and reporting back.

8. Have a record made of the assignments given and items to be followed up on. Who will do what, and when?

9. Consider both ministering and administering, with emphasis on ministering. *Administering* tends to focus on programs, activities, and meetings. *Ministering,* on the other hand, focuses on people and principles first, and then programs are considered in the context of how best to serve the people and teach the principles.

   Without careful attention to ministering, it is easy to be consumed by the details of administering. If attention in a meeting is given entirely to staffing, budgeting, calendaring, planning, scheduling, and programming, we might be doing things right, but may not be getting the right things done. If the needs of people take second place or are left out, we can be busily engaged in a multitude of good things that can distract us from the few things that make all the difference. In a well-planned meeting, first things are placed first.

Conducting a Meeting

It is the responsibility of the one conducting the meeting to ensure as far as possible that the purpose for the meeting is accomplished, thus making it a good meeting, "better than no meeting at all." Several aspects of conducting an effective meeting follow:

Preparing in advance. Leaders should review and be familiar with each item on the agenda. Consideration should be given for the climate, environment, and setting for the meeting. This responsibility may be delegated, but there should be a comfortable setting and access to any materials or equipment needed. Table, chairs, chalkboard, scriptures, handbooks, and other items should be in place before the meeting begins. This is important to establish a feeling of order, preparation, readiness, and anticipation as people arrive.

Managing the meeting. The leader conducting the meeting is responsible to "manage" the meeting. This is done by keeping the focus on the purpose for the meeting. Out of respect for everyone involved, a responsible leader will move through the agenda and close the meeting at the designated time. It may be necessary to carry some items over to a later time.

Leading a discussion. An effective leader will encourage participation when a discussion is appropriate. As has been said, "Information leads to inspiration," and a discussion can provide information. Some pointers for leading an effective discussion:

1. Identify and clarify the purpose for the discussion.

2. Give some indication of the time allotted for the discussion. Setting this expectation up in advance helps keep things under control and allows the leader to terminate the discussion without offending someone who might otherwise feel cut off when the time is up.

3. Ask a secretary or other appropriate person to take notes of major points to be followed up on and points to be covered in summarizing the discussion at the conclusion.

4. Ask questions that invite participation and understanding, such as:
   What is your feeling?
   How do you see it?
   What has been your experience?
   Will you share your insight?
   Is there a difference of opinion that
      could shed light on this matter?

> How might this suggestion help
> bring souls unto Christ?
> In what ways will this contribute
> to the mission of the Church?

Note: If there are those in the group who are less apt to participate, it is well to draw them out by inviting their comments. When the leader demonstrates active listening and gives brief acknowledgment to comments, it encourages those who might normally be less likely to contribute.

Listening. The message of the Savior in the first verse of the Doctrine and Covenants speaks to us of listening together: "Hearken, O ye people of my church, saith the voice of him who dwells on high, and whose eyes are upon all men; yea, verily I say: Hearken ye people from afar; and ye that are upon the islands of the sea, listen together" (D&C 1:1).

When we learn to listen to the whisperings of the Spirit, we are better prepared to listen to one another with discernment and understanding. There is more to listening than just hearing what is being said. A leader who has developed the skill of active listening encourages meaningful discussion by:

1. Giving close attention and listening with the ears and heart for the purpose of gaining information and understanding.

2. Asking for further clarification that invites a deeper sensitivity to what is being said.

3. Resisting the impulse to talk unless it is to help clarify or ask questions that invite understanding and participation.

4. Avoiding the temptation to express his or her own thoughts and opinions too soon in response to comments. This tends to discourage some from making their contribution.

Concluding the discussion. At the conclusion of a discussion, the discussion leader may:

1. Ask someone who has been notified in advance to make a summary statement of the main points discussed.

2. Invite any final comments that might lead to clarification.

3. Acknowledge and express appreciation for the time and contribution of those present.

4. Make decisions on what is to be done and follow up on how those decisions will be implemented.

COUNCIL MEETINGS

Today there is an increased emphasis on the importance of the council system: ward councils, stake councils, and all other means of counseling together. The idea of councils is not new to our thinking. It harks clear back to the great Council in Heaven, which we attended as spirit children of our Heavenly Father.

In an effectively working council, men and women share the vision and are united on what they want to have happen. Having a sense of ownership encourages the commitment to become part of the solution, not part of the problem. Members draw from each other's experience and inspiration, and in the process everyone grows.

One of the great benefits of council meetings is that they bring together the resources of all the organizations to meet the needs of individuals. Effective leadership can unite a group so everyone is aiming at the same target. Using the analogy of basketball, consider what the score might be if every player were shooting in his or her own separate basket. For example, suppose the Relief Society president attending a ward council meeting was focused only on the basket for the Relief Society organization. She might wait patiently until the subject of Relief

Society was to be addressed before becoming involved. The same might happen with the Young Women and Primary presidents, each with her own separate basket, agenda, area of responsibility and accountability, and loyalty to her organization.

In a council meeting where the needs of individuals are concerned, and the resources available cross organizational lines, and everyone is shooting at the same basket, so to speak, the score is very high. Let me give an actual example of a ward council meeting in which each participant focused on individual needs in a spirit of unity and sharing.

First, my mother, who was living with my husband and me, was confined to a wheelchair and often expressed her feelings of despair at not being useful or needed anymore. Our church building was up the hill from where we lived. My husband, a stake president at the time, was seldom available to assist on Sunday mornings by either lifting the wheelchair into the car or pushing it up the hill. The Relief Society president was aware of and felt some concern for our problem, and brought it to the council.

Second, in our ward, the bishop's Primary-age son had some behavior problems that were very disruptive to his class and prevented the teacher from presenting her lesson. The class members were not being taught and the bishop's son was not having the individual attention he needed to help him control his behavior. The Primary president had a concern.

In the Mia Maid class, a young woman who had made some serious mistakes had chosen to separate herself from her family and from the Church. Her attitude reflected her feelings of being unaccepted, unappreciated, and of no value. Her welfare was the concern of the Young Women leader. The following account tells what can happen when, counseling together, each person with a specific concern is willing to reach out to others, regardless of the organization. The goal—to help an individual—was the common denominator for everyone present.

One evening, one of the leaders from that meeting called to see if it would be all right to come to our home and issue a call to my mother. Of course he could come, but I was a little curious as to what the call might be. And when I explained to my mother that someone was coming to issue a call to her, her first reaction was one of concern. "What could they possibly want of me?" was her comment. And then it seemed she became rejuvenated, anticipating the visit. It had been a number of years since she had received a calling in the Church. She must have been thinking, "Am I really needed? Is there something I can do to be useful, to contribute?"

The leader came, and we visited briefly. Then he leaned forward in his chair and directed his comments to my mother. "Sister Greene," he said, "in the Primary there is a young boy who needs someone to sit right next to him and help him have proper conduct. We need you and he needs you." Then he issued the call. "We are calling you to be a companion to Bradley [not his real name]. We would like to have you sit in your wheelchair right at the end of the row and be responsible for helping Bradley each Sunday. We would hope you might develop a relationship with him so that he would respond to the love that you could give him, and thus help this young boy, the teacher in the class, and the class members. We feel you would be very successful in this calling. Would you accept it?" He clearly identified what they hoped would happen. After only a moment, my mother responded: "Well, if you think I can do that, I'll do my best."

At about the same time, I learned that the young Mia Maid who would not attend church or associate with the young women her age had accepted an assignment to come on Sunday mornings and help me push my mother in her wheelchair up the hill to church. Although there were many things she refused to do, she was willing to push that wheelchair.

And what happened when these inspired leaders in a ward council focused first on the needs of individuals, crossing organizational lines to find the resources available to meet all the needs?

My mom sat by Bradley each Sunday morning, giving him the love and concern that she would have shown for her own grandson. This was especially wonderful for her because she had no grandchildren living close by. She began talking to him about his mission, and at the close of each class when his behavior was good, she gave him twenty-five cents for his missionary fund. I recently heard this young boy, a grown man now who has fulfilled a mission, tell about how Sister Greene loved him and believed in him as a child and affected his life in a remarkable way.

The young woman, Shauna [not her real name], who was given the calling to push the wheelchair, became like a granddaughter to my mother, who loved her like her own, knowing nothing about Shauna's mistakes or questionable conduct. This young woman attended church because, as she said, "Sister Greene needs me." After my mother passed away, this young woman, whose reactivation began by pushing a wheelchair, told how she visited my mother's grave regularly and took a flower in appreciation for the love she had felt when it was so desperately needed.

After her calling, my mother lived each week with renewed enthusiasm in anticipation of the special goal she had to help Bradley "be a good boy."

When leaders counsel together in meetings where needs and resources are brought together, when there is a unity in what they want to have happen, when concern for individuals comes before programs, and when resources are made available across organizational lines to meet the needs, miracles can happen.

The most effective councils are those in which every person's input is valued. A father shared with me the outcome of a family council in which his family determined together to develop a family mission statement and a motto. Each member participated in the council, making recommendations and contributing to the discussion. It became the unanimous decision of the council that the recommendation of the eight-year-old, even though there were teenagers with more experience, was ideal for their family. The motto selected was, "Do what is right no matter what." Would that simple motto from a Primary child be considered inspirational? I think so.

Elder M. Russell Ballard, in his book *Counseling with Our Councils,* provides valuable, practical, and detailed information and insight on the purpose for councils, how they work, how they are to be conducted, and how to prepare for participating in councils for the purpose of accomplishing the Lord's work. He explains: "Each council member has a responsibility to be spiritually in tune when taking part in council meetings so that he or she can make a positive contribution to the issues being discussed. . . . As we do this, our councils will be conducted in a spirit of love and compassion and will follow the example of the Lord, who 'counseleth in wisdom, and in justice, and in great mercy' (Jacob 4:10)" (*Counseling with Our Councils,* p. 66).

When I anticipate attending a council meeting with priesthood leaders, I have found it helpful to prepare in advance a written note or memo to help clarify my thoughts on items that I know will be presented, or that I am to report back on in my area of responsibility. This process has improved my ability to be specific, to the point, and focused on what matters most. In this memo, I try to organize my thoughts in three areas: (1) observation, (2) concern, (3) recommendation.

1. Observation: In my area of responsibility, what do I see or feel that would be relevant to this meeting and require the awareness and attention of the council? Many, perhaps even most, of the details for implementing a program should not require the attention of the full council. But matters pertaining to ministering to individuals and families reach across organizational lines. Such matters are best attended to with all of the resources available within the council, where needs and resources can be matched.

2. Concern: What things might be interfering with or preventing "what we want to have happen" in the lives of individuals and families, particularly those in the organization I represent? There are many concerns, just as there are many needs, but careful preparation and thought will provide a way of determining those of highest priority, so that what matters most is not left undone.

3. Recommendation: A council meeting is not a place for dumping problems but for solving them. Based on the information that is available through study, counsel, and prayer, I come to the council meeting prepared with my best recommendation for what might be considered in the process of meeting needs and solving problems. In view of the overall picture, the insight gained through counseling together, and the direction from priesthood leaders, my recommendation may be accepted, modified, or completely disregarded in the final decision. I have found on occasion that what I thought was a good idea was not accepted. Then I have learned later that the idea was good but the timing was off. Someday the idea would be not only right but timely.

The satisfaction of participating in a council meeting does not depend on our contribution being accepted, but rather on whether we were prepared to give helpful counsel in view of our insight and responsibilities. If so, we can feel that our participation has been important. The question is never *who* is right, but rather *what* is right. And as the old saying goes, "A lot can be accomplished if we don't care who gets the credit."

Many times I have found that the most valuable benefit of counseling together is not what we bring to the meeting, but rather what we take from the meeting. When we prepare our hearts and minds to listen for information and understanding, we can learn from others and increase our effectiveness.

In conclusion, as we consider the meetings we must attend, conduct, and follow through on in our callings as women leaders in the Church, let us not neglect the most important meeting we participate in: sacrament meeting. This is the weekly meeting that can strengthen our spirituality and help prepare us for all other responsibilities in the home, in the Church, and in life generally. Effective leadership depends on being guided by the Spirit in all matters pertaining to the needs of individuals and families. It is in the weekly sacrament meeting that we partake of the sacrament and renew our covenants in remembrance of him whose work we are engaged in. We covenant to keep the commandments so we can have his Spirit to be with us. Having the Spirit of the Lord is the single most important part of our calling—more important than skills, experience, maturity, or natural ability. Recognizing, feeling, and following the promptings of the Spirit should be the matter of greatest importance in all leadership responsibility.

Consider the words to the hymn "We Meet Again As Sisters" (*Hymns*, no. 311):

> *We meet again as sisters*
> *On this the Sabbath day*
> *To worship God together,*
> *To testify and pray.*
> *Now may the Holy Spirit,*
> *Descending like a dove,*
> *Enlarge our minds with knowledge*
> *And fill our hearts with love.*

May this Spirit attend all our meetings as we lead, guide, and walk beside each other in our various responsibilities. With minds enlarged with knowledge and hearts filled with love, we can go forward with confidence in the work of the Lord.

CHAPTER SEVEN

TIME MANAGEMENT

*We are as anxious for women to be wise in the
management of their time as we are for them to be wise
stewards of the family's storehouse of food.*
PRESIDENT SPENCER W. KIMBALL

"I do not have time." Is that a phrase you have ever spoken aloud or thought in private? Is there any sister in the Church who does not say this, or at least feel on occasion the impact of not having enough time to do all that she needs or wants to do? Whether you lead, guide, or walk beside, leadership requires time. Does the feeling of being too busy ever plague you? Have you experienced a yearning desire to avoid being overwhelmed or underwhelmed, but rather just "whelmed" . . . balanced, ordered, in control?

Time management is an essential element of effective leadership, and it can be learned. I recall years ago telling my mother how very busy I was, hoping for a little sympathy or at least her acknowledgment of my dedication to something that was consuming my time. She listened attentively and then responded with these words, "I am sure you are busy, but you know, my dear, it doesn't take much to keep some people busy." That thought had never occurred to me. Yes, we can be very busy doing things without ever really getting the right things done.

In his address "Jesus, the Perfect Leader," President Spencer W. Kimball spoke of the wise use of time. "Jesus also taught us how important it is to use our time wisely. This does not mean there can never be any leisure, for there must be time for contemplation and for renewal, but there must be no waste of time. How we manage time matters so very much, and we can be good managers of time without being frantic or officious. Time cannot be recycled. When a moment has gone, it is really gone. The tyranny of trivia consists of its driving out the people and moments that really matter. Minutia holds momentous things hostage, and we let the tyranny continue all too often. Wise time management is really the wise management of ourselves" (*Ensign*, August 1979, p. 6).

Brigham Young said, "What have we? Our time. Spend it as you will. Time is given to you; and when this is spent to the best possible advantage for promoting truth upon the earth, it is placed to our account, and blessed are you; but when we spend our time in idleness and folly it will be placed against us" (*Discourses of Brigham Young,* comp. John A. Widtsoe [Salt Lake City: Deseret Book, 1975], p. 290).

In response to the comment, "I do not have time," we must understand that we have all there is. With twenty-four hours a day allotted to every person, what is the magic that holds some people captive and frees others to use time more efficiently and thus become more effective leaders? We need to understand time, what it is and how to manage it. This will free us from the stress that seems to be so much a part of our society and contributes to our feelings of being overwhelmed.

Albert Einstein explained, "Time is the occurrence of events one after another." An "event" is any happening, as global as putting a man on the moon or as intimate as the blink of an eye. Wise time management comes through identifying the events in our lives that we can control and adapting to those we cannot.

While time-management principles can be helpful in all phases of our lives, as leaders we have an increased responsibility for the wise use of time, not only for ourselves but for those with whom we work and serve. Because our time is our life, it is well when making plans to consider the questions, What will be the possible benefits or return for the investment of my time or the time of those who serve under my leadership? Is this project a worthy use of our time? Will this investment of time move us toward or away from our ultimate goal or desired outcome?

To the question, How do you do it all? the answer should be, I don't. I plan with a purpose, I prioritize, I delegate. One mother of a large family, when asked how she managed to do it all, explained that she worked by the method of select and neglect. "I select what I am going to neglect so that I don't neglect what I have chosen to select."

So how do we make the most of our time and get the greatest return from time invested? We do it by planning, by setting goals. Time management and goal setting are inseparable. But it is the responsibility of the leader to help identify valued, prioritized goals. When we prioritize, it becomes obvious that decorations, for example, although nice, are not essential if they are created at the expense of time that could be spent in going after the one or including the ninety and nine. On the other hand, with proper planning, the decorations could serve a useful purpose by providing a way to involve others and allow them to use their talents and to form friendships.

Another skill in the wise use of time is to learn to deal with vital tasks before they become urgent. Here is a simple way to understand the difference between urgent and vital tasks: When you were in school and you knew you had a term paper due at the end of the month, was the assignment vital to your success in school? The answer, of course, is yes. When did that task become urgent? Too often the answer is the week before or maybe even the night before the paper was due. It is putting off the vital until it becomes urgent that brings on a sense of stress, a feeling of being out of control and under pressure.

Planning in advance provides an opportunity to get an early start and avoid the stress. It leaves time to ponder, to receive inspiration, to consider alternatives, and to accommodate for disappointment when things may not work out as planned. When something is vital, it is important not to delay until it becomes urgent. Yes, it is important to respond when things are urgent, but most things will not come to that point if we plan in advance.

Charles E. Hummel explains: "The [vital] task rarely must

be done today or even this week. The urgent task calls for instant action. The momentary appeal of these tasks seems irresistible and they devour our energy. But in the light of time's perspective, their deceptive prominence fades. With a sense of loss we recall the vital task we pushed aside, and we realize we have become slaves to the tyranny of the urgent" (Charles R. Hobbs, *Insight of Time Management* n.p.: Charles R. Hobbs Corp., 1977], p. 7).

When we distinguish between the urgent and the vital, we have a sense of being in control instead of being controlled by the pressure of urgency. Dealing with vital tasks before they become urgent is an important leadership skill.

Another attribute of a successful leader is punctuality. Think what it really means to be punctual, on time, never late, never tardy—in meetings, reports, expectations, responsibilities, deadlines, or decisions.

A leader conducting a meeting should not wait for late-comers, but in consideration for those who come on time must begin on time. One who comes late when it can be avoided, which is most of the time, is insensitive to the time of others.

Planning ahead is important to punctuality. I learned this important lesson years ago while serving as a counselor in the Young Women general presidency. There was a meeting scheduled Sunday morning at 7:00 A.M. in the office of the Presiding Bishopric. I had certainly intended to leave in plenty of time to ensure my punctuality. But on the spur of the moment I decided to make a minor revision in a document I was going to present. I left a few minutes later than intended, but determined to accommodate for my poor judgment by going a bit above the speed limit on a less-traveled road. Surely on a Sunday morning with little traffic there would be no concern.

I was only a few blocks from my home when I heard the police siren. My heart sank. I pulled over to the side of the road, and as the officer approached me I began explaining my urgent situation, that I had a meeting with the Presiding Bishopric and must not be late. He smiled as if to say, "Yes, I'll bet you do," but simply wrote down my license number and motioned me on.

I had an overwhelming feeling of gratitude as I made my way to the Church Office Building, parked, and hurried to the elevator. My heart was pounding as I waited for the doors to open. Catching my breath and my composure, I walked into the meeting only a moment late. Everyone was smiling and greeted me warmly. Then someone revealed their reason for such a warm greeting, explaining, "We understand you had a police escort." I was embarrassed, to say the least. The policeman had called ahead to confirm that my plea was valid, thus revealing much more than I would have liked. My late arrival gave me more attention than I ever expected or wanted.

In discussing my embarrassment, someone explained to me a great principle about punctuality. He said, "When you are only ten minutes early, you are five minutes late." Consideration of this principle has served me well over the years, and many opportunities to discuss matters of importance and gain helpful information have come during that valuable window of time before the meeting begins.

Joseph Smith once had this article about George Washington published for the Church members in Nauvoo: "President Washington was the most punctual man in the observance of appointments ever known to the writer. He delivered his communications to Congress at the opening of each session, in person. He always appointed the hour of twelve for this purpose, and he never failed to enter the hall of Congress while the state-house clock was stricking that hour. His invitations for dinner were always given for four o'clock P.M. He allowed five minutes for variation of time pieces, and he waited no longer for anyone. Certain lagging members of Congress sometimes came in when the dinner was nearly half over. The writer has heard the President say to them with a smile, 'gentlemen we are too punctual for you—I have a cook who never asks whether the company has come, but whether the hour has come'" (*Times and Seasons,* 2:270).

Why was this article published to the Saints? Is it possible that the Spirit of the Lord, having labored well ahead of time to prepare for the meeting, is the cook who begins serving at the appointed hour? Are others of us His assistant cooks? Isn't it right to begin on time when many have sacrificed to be there?

Another key in time management is to recognize procrastination as a thief of time. Procrastination can hold us captive in prison walls of our own making. With procrastination comes indecision, the disease that is sometimes referred to as the "paralysis of analysis." Time spent in study, prayer, deliberation, counsel, and thoughtful reflection is vital, but delaying a decision unnecessarily or failing to take action where appropriate is avoiding responsibility. This little rhyme states the problem clearly:

> *Procrastination is a terrible thing,*
> *It only causes sorrow.*
> *But I can stop at any time;*
> *I think I will—tomorrow.*

The best way to avoid procrastination is to have a plan of action that discourages it and creates within you a sense of anticipation. Give yourself a time frame and a commitment, a deadline. Allow for flexibility. Don't use the drive for perfection—which can masquerade as a virtue—as a delay tactic. Reduce overwhelming projects into bite-size portions. While working through the process, keep ever in mind the desired outcome that is worthy of your time and effort. Avoid rationalizing, telling yourself, "I do not have time." Remember, we have all there is.

It may be time for us to consider looking at the time wasters that plague our lives. Try keeping a record for a day or two of precisely where your time is going, thus revealing the culprits that become thieves of time. Such logs usually reveal that time wasters fall into patterns that are repeated over and over. Once we are aware of them, we can change the habits that devour our time.

Some time wasters are self-imposed habits that can be changed. If you do not take enough time for planning—change. In the case of ineffective delegation—change. Attempting too much without prioritizing—change. Too much involvement in details—change. Lack of self-discipline—change. Chronic lateness—change. Procrastination—change. Unwillingness to terminate visits—change. Failure to anticipate—change.

Habits can be changed. Consider the message in the following essay titled *Habit* by an unknown author:

I am your constant companion
I am your greatest helper or heaviest burden
I will push you onward or drag you down to failure
I am completely at your command
Half the things you do you might just as well turn over to me
And I will be able to do them quickly and correctly
I am easily managed, you must merely be firm with me
Show me exactly how you want something done and
    after a few lessons I will do it automatically
I am the servant of all great men and alas, of all failures as well
Those who are great I have made great
Those who are failures I have made failures
I am not a machine, though I work with the precision of a machine
Plus the intelligence of man
You may run me for profit or run me for ruin
It makes no difference to me
Take me, train me, be firm with me, and
    I will place the world at your feet
Be easy with me and I will destroy you
Who am I? I am Habit.

Here is some food for thought: "If you keep doing what you're doing, you will keep getting what you're getting." In evaluating our present effectiveness, it would be well to keep in mind the words of the old farmer who, when asked how he was doing, responded, "I'm better'n I was but I ain't as good as I'm gonna be."

Time is a precious commodity that can be used or abused. A calling to leadership can be lengthy or brief, but while the opportunity exists, the wise management of time is a sacred trust.

CHAPTER EIGHT

DELEGATION

❧

And Moses chose able men out of all Israel,
and made them heads over the people, rulers of thousands,
rulers of hundreds, rulers of fifties, and rulers of tens.
And they judged the people at all seasons:
the hard causes they brought unto Moses,
but every small matter they judged themselves.
EXODUS 18:25-26

I was once invited to a ward Relief Society visiting teaching convention in a distant location. I received a creative, handmade invitation giving the details of the event, to which all the sisters of that ward were invited. The night of the convention, I arrived at the church building about fifteen minutes early and was greeted at the door by the Relief Society president. Her counselors, she explained, were finishing up details in the kitchen.

The cultural hall had been divided with panels to provide a warm feeling. The setting was a display of artistic excellence, the walls and panels covered with handmade floral designs of every imaginable flower interlaced with ivy in various shades of green and yellow. It was explained to me that the daughter of one of the presidency members had spent hours creating this marvelous display. It was splendid, beautiful, and very impressive.

Within this area were round tables with matching floral cloths, and in the center of each table were eight small jars of homemade jam made by the presidency, each with a floral doily tied with a ribbon around the top—gifts for the guests who would be sitting at that table.

The presidency appeared to me to be weary, yet warm and enthusiastic in anticipation of the evening and all who would be in attendance. At about ten after seven, when only a few sisters had arrived, there were comments about Mormon Standard Time and what might be going on at school that night to delay some of the mothers from getting there on time. The few who had arrived gathered in one corner around two tables, and we visited while we waited and waited. The Relief Society president returned frequently to the door in anticipation of latecomers.

At the end of the evening, which closed early, there were lots of leftovers, bottles of jam not picked up, and a deep sense of disappointment on the part of the presidency. Here they had spent hours and hours to make this evening special, and only a few sisters had shown up. Only a few were there to appreciate or even be aware of the sacrifice of time and energy expended in hopes of serving so many.

The presidency cleaned up the tables that hadn't been used and went home feeling exhausted, disappointed, and probably "burned out." It is an interesting phenomenon that when something that requires great effort accomplishes the intended aim, fatigue is replaced with exhilaration and enthusiasm and sometimes even anticipation of the next opportunity for participating in such an event. That was not the case on this disappointing evening.

I'm sure this example is a bit unusual and maybe extreme, but there are some leadership principles to be learned from these dedicated, disappointed leaders.

What might have happened if, in the beginning of the planning, those diligent sisters had spent less time on the physical arrangement and more on figuring out how each sister might be involved, how the less active might have received a personal contact, and how the principle of delegation might have provided opportunities for sharing and serving and a feeling of being needed? The Relief Society presidency would not have been in the kitchen. They would have been on hand to lead, guide, and walk beside, setting the example for future leaders as others were given the opportunity to serve.

President Spencer W. Kimball taught, "You cannot do both your own work and your subordinates' work. . . . [Ask,] 'Is this something I must do, or could it be done by others?'" (*The Teachings of Spencer W. Kimball* [Salt Lake City: Bookcraft, 1982], p. 488). Delegation in the Church involves much more than getting a job done. In fact, sometimes an assignment properly delegated serves as the means of developing leadership for those involved, which may in the long run be more important than the immediate task, job, or activity. Over the years I have had many opportunities, even at a very young age, to benefit from leaders who have trusted me with responsibilities that have caused me to reach and stretch. In the process I have learned that leaders who are effective in helping to train other leaders know when to lead, when to guide, and when to walk beside.

President Spencer W. Kimball, in his article "Jesus, the Perfect Leader," taught some important principles of delegation:

"Jesus knew how to involve his disciples in the process of life. He gave them important and specific things to do for their development. Other leaders have sought to be so omnicompetent that they have tried to do everything themselves, which produces little growth in others. Jesus trusts his followers enough to share his work with them so that they can grow. That is one of the greatest lessons of his leadership. If we brush other people aside in order to see a task done more quickly and effectively, the task may get done all right, but without the growth and development in followers that is so important. Because Jesus knows that this life is purposeful and that we have been placed on this planet in order to perform and grow, growth then becomes one of the great ends of life as well as a means. We can give correct feedback to others in a loving and helpful way when mistakes are made.

"Jesus was not afraid to make demands of those he led. His leadership was not condescending or soft. He had the courage to call Peter and others to leave their fishing nets and to follow him, not after the fishing season or after the next catch, but now! today! Jesus let people know that he believed in them and in their possibilities, and thus he was free to help them stretch their souls in fresh achievement" (*Ensign,* August 1979, p. 6).

Where effective delegation takes place there are many benefits:

1. Delegation multiplies the resources.
2. Delegation develops leadership skills in others.
3. Delegation strengthens and builds the whole organization.
4. Delegation distributes the workload, leaving the leader free to do the things only he or she can do.
5. Delegation creates a climate for teamwork.
6. Delegation builds confidence and a feeling of worth, a feeling critical to a person's sense of well-being: "I'm needed—I'm valuable—I can contribute."

Delegation is more effective when planning with a purpose has taken place, when you have decided what you want to have happen, keeping always in mind that the ultimate purpose for all of our work is to strengthen testimony and bring souls unto Christ. As a leader, you may sometimes be looking for the person most experienced, the one most qualified, the one who knows the most about the activity. This would certainly be the case if you were conducting a CPR class, for example, teaching skills to be used in case of an emergency. On the other hand, if part of the purpose is to provide opportunity for others to grow in leadership responsibility, you might delegate the ward talent show to someone who may be less experienced or younger or less active. The key to effective delegation is for the one who is delegating to know the task and know the people who might be called to serve.

Consider what might happen if this were not the case.

Suppose a leader does not know the task, hasn't planned with a purpose, and doesn't know the sisters she has to work with—their talents, their needs, their interest or experience. In this situation there is no chance for effective delegation. A vague assignment may be dumped, but it will likely result in disappointment and maybe discouragement on the part of those involved.

Perhaps the leader has a good knowledge of her people but hasn't clearly defined the task to be done. This can be a problem. She may be asking someone she knows to be responsible for something she is not able to clarify. This too can cause frustration for the leader and also the one being called to serve.

What if a task has been well planned with a purpose, but the leader doesn't really know the people well? The leader may have clearly in mind what is desired and may even have explained the guidelines completely, thus having high expectations. But not knowing the sisters being asked to serve, she might not be aware that one sister has had no experience and has no support from home, another has major responsibilities demanding her time, and another may be in poor health, thus preventing her from accomplishing what is expected even though she may accept the assignment. Thus, the leader is disappointed in her expectation, and the sister being asked to serve feels that she has failed and has disappointed others. What if a sister, for various reasons, is not able to carry the full responsibility because of lack of experience or time or resources, but would benefit from the participation? A wise leader, knowing her sisters, would extend the delegation to be shared with another sister with more experience or time, and working together could be a positive experience for all involved.

The best possible case, of course, is when the leader knows the task and knows the people. She is then prepared to delegate in the most effective way. She can describe the purpose of the delegated task and what is to be accomplished, with confidence that those who are being asked to participate will be both willing and able.

When the tasks and the people have been appropriately matched, the following suggested steps in delegation can take place, remembering that the most qualified person may not always be the right person:

1. Ask the person to accept the responsibility for a specific assignment, explaining the total project and the desired outcome.

2. Share guidelines relating to the assignment, such things as budget restrictions, available resources, time constraints, and other items as appropriate.

3. Explain the importance of this assignment in the overall objective of the leadership plan, which ultimately is to strengthen testimony and bring souls unto Christ.

4. Ask the person to accept the assignment and allow her to share her thoughts on how it might be carried out.

5. Decide together when the assignment is to be completed.

6. Explain that reporting back is vital and should be as frequent as needed, according to the experience of the individual and the complexity of the assignment. Reporting back provides an opportunity to encourage, clarify, teach, nurture, and counsel with those less experienced. In the case of confident, experienced people, it may simply provide a way for all to be informed so there are fewer surprises and more opportunities to express gratitude, appreciation, and encouragement. In all cases there should be an agreed-upon date or dates

for when the one receiving the assignment should
return and report.

7. When proper delegation takes place, how the
assignment is to be accomplished is best left up to
the one given the responsibility. When someone is
told *what* needs to be accomplished, rather than *how*
it should be done, it increases a sense of trust and
responsibility and provides an opportunity for the
one accepting the assignment to seek inspiration
and pray for guidance. Delegation capitalizes on the
inspiration and leadership of others, relieving the
president of the working out of the plan, even
though she carries the responsibility and must be
accountable to the one to whom she reports. It is
interesting to note that, at every level of
responsibility, everyone has someone he or she is
accountable to, someone to report back to.

My mind goes back to the initial planning of the first
Young Women Worldwide Celebration. Months and months
before the event, consideration was given to the idea of some
activity that would help young women throughout the world
feel part of a mighty force for righteousness in a shared experience.

We began by using planning with a purpose for a guide.
The values were in place, and the purpose for all our experiences was to help young women prepare to make and keep
sacred covenants and receive the ordinances of the temple. It
was determined that the plan should include experiences that
would strengthen testimony, create a feeling of worldwide sisterhood, and enhance feelings of responsibility to share the
gospel and to bear testimony. There was no question that there
would be support for what we wanted to have happen. The
question was how to accomplish this worthy objective. The
guidelines included some restrictions that might have been dis-
couraging in a normal situation.

When the assignment was delegated, the guidelines imposed involved the following limitations: There must be minimal or no travel beyond stake boundaries; there must be minimal expense; the event or the experience must be universal in nature, appropriate to all young women in every corner of the world; the event was to be held within the coming year. A committee was appointed. They were given the purpose and the guidelines and invited to come forward with a plan that would accomplish the purpose within the guidelines.

The committee began to work, utilizing all the resources they could imagine. Many times the committee reported back, testing ideas, making recommendations, reevaluating possibilities, throwing out some ideas and refining others, seeking information and inspiration. After months of refinement, the plan was finally in place within all the established guidelines. The final report was made on schedule. The plan was approved. The assignment was then delegated or communicated to all of the ward, branch, and stake leaders throughout the entire Church.

On October 11, 1986, young women met at daybreak in branches, wards, and stakes all over the world. They wrote statements of their personal testimonies of the gospel of Jesus Christ on small cards and attached them to helium-filled balloons. And, with the help of the wind in most areas, testimonies of the young women were released to the world.

Elder Lance B. Wickham of Poway, California, who was then serving as stake president, wrote of this activity: "It was one of the most inspiring youth activities I have ever witnessed. The great moment came as dozens of brightly colored balloons, each with a sweet, simple handwritten testimony of a young woman fastened to it, ascended skyward. We watched transfixed as the balloons floated steadily heavenward until they disappeared into the clouds still gathered overhead. I cannot express the feeling that I felt, that we all felt at that moment."

Did this activity accomplish the purpose for which it was

planned? The response was overwhelming. One young woman from Anchorage, Alaska, wrote on her card, "I am fifteen years old and a member of The Church of Jesus Christ of Latter-day Saints. I know that God lives and loves us. Jesus Christ is the Savior of the world. I love them with all my heart. If I could wish for anything for the world I would wish that everyone had a sure knowledge that God lives and that He hears and answers prayers. I am thankful for the answers I have received to my prayers. You too can receive answers to your prayers. All you have to do is ask. No matter who you are or what you have done, God will listen." Such messages led individuals, and in at least one case an entire family, to seek out the missionaries and learn about the Church.

Following every event that we plan with a purpose, it is important that we take time to evaluate, asking, Did what we want to have happen, happen? When an assignment is delegated, the responsibility for that outcome is given to those who accepted the assignment. In this case, they had performed within guidelines, with inspiration and creativity, and yes, even with the help of the wind on that day. In our evaluation meeting we all agreed that what we wanted to have happen had indeed happened.

Understanding how important and effective delegation can be, why would we ever hesitate to do it? Here are some common obstacles that may help us better understand and overcome our reluctance:

I feel I can do it better myself. I'm more
experienced and ultimately I am responsible.

Maybe you can do it better, but can someone else do it well enough and have the opportunity to learn, even if it puts at risk your reputation for superior quality?

It takes too much time to train someone else.

Yes, effective delegation does take time, but time is not the only consideration. You must also consider whether this provides an opportunity to train someone who can then train another and another.

I lack confidence in the person's ability
or dependability or availability.

Identify specific reasons for your feelings. Are they justified? If so, delegate a different assignment, or include an assistant with more experience who will help the less experienced one.

I won't get the credit or recognition or praise.

A bit of this feeling may be normal, but effective leaders will focus on what can be accomplished through others and for others.

But I enjoy doing it.

Continue doing some things just because you like them, but if you allow yourself to grow by learning to let go, in the process everyone grows. Growth is often painful, but it's always worthwhile.

I'm not sure what to delegate and what not to delegate.

When you know your people and you know the task, you can delegate almost everything except confidential matters and authority for modifying policies or established procedures.

An old proverb says, "Many hands make light work." This is true only if those hands are able to contribute in an effective way to what needs to be accomplished. Perhaps you are aware of situations where in the name of delegation a job or an assignment has been "dumped." The result has been disappointing to the one who assigned the job and the one who was intended to carry it out. Make sure every task you delegate is worthy of a person's best efforts.

In summary:

1. Know your purpose, what it is you want
   to have happen.

2. Know your people, their strengths, their weaknesses, their goals, and their desires.

3. Remember that the "right" person may not always be the one most qualified. Leadership involves developing leaders.

4. Establish expectations and deadlines and guidelines.

5. Establish a reporting procedure.

6. Follow up. It is helpful to write a memo summarizing the delegated project. This provides an opportunity to stress the person's responsibility for the task. It also helps clarify expectations and prevent any misunderstanding.

Compliment the person throughout the process of accomplishing the task, and review work on a regularly scheduled timetable. Give feedback, evaluation, and constructive suggestions. Finally, always give the person credit for success, but in the case of seeming failure, accept the responsibility yourself.

Through proper delegation, everyone can be involved. As Eliza R. Snow, the second general president of the Relief Society, said, "There is no sister so isolated, and her sphere so narrow but what she can do a great deal towards establishing the Kingdom of God upon the earth" (*Woman's Exponent,* September 15, 1873, p. 62).

CHAPTER NINE

COUNSELORS

*Wherefore, now let every man learn his duty, and to act
in the office in which he is appointed, in all diligence.*
D&C 107:99

I learned an important lesson some years ago when I was called as a counselor to Sister Ruth Funk, who had just been called to be the general Young Women president. I was much less experienced than she, less known, less confident. I felt anxious about this calling. Adding to my concern, Sister Funk explained to me that she wouldn't have requested that I be called to be her counselor, because she didn't know me that well. We had had little opportunity to work together or associate together and didn't live in the same neighborhood or town. Then she taught me this important lesson. "Ardeth," she said, "the Lord called you." Her testimony of my calling was a tremendous blessing to me, and it helped sustain me until I received my own confirmation of the Lord's will concerning this call. It was a great blessing to me that the president with whom I was to serve could bear testimony of having been guided by the Spirit in recommending me as her counselor.

Counselors are called by priesthood leaders, those in authority, but it is the president's responsibility to seek the Lord's will in earnest prayer and to nominate two counselors. This decision usually needs to be made in a relatively short period of time after the call. I remember my own experience when I was called as general Young Women president and was asked to submit the names of two women for consideration as my counselors. There are often feelings of loneliness in leadership, and I remember experiencing such feelings as I considered the importance of this decision. Counsel of other trusted leaders can be helpful in making decisions, but the inspiration for choosing counselors comes to the president, not to a neighbor, a friend, or even a family member.

There is a pattern provided for this important decision, and when it is followed, a feeling of peace and confidence replaces uncertainty and indecision. "But, behold, I say unto you, that you must study it out in your mind; then you must ask me if it be right, and if it is right I will cause that your bosom shall burn within you; therefore, you shall feel that it is right" (D&C 9:8).

This pattern is for every leader, at every level of experience. One young woman, Melanie, tells about her decision process: "I was called to be a class president of seventeen girls, and the bishop said I was responsible for them. I was scared to death. I didn't even know for sure who they were. Then he told me to decide on my counselors and to pray and ask the Lord. I wondered how it worked—how would I know whom the Lord wanted.

"I wrote seventeen names on a piece of paper. Then I prayed about those names. Each time I would finish my prayer, I felt right about crossing off one or two names from the list. I kept thinking and praying and trying to decide until the third day. With only two names remaining, I had a strong feeling that I knew whom Heavenly Father wanted. That's how it works."

There may be some occasions when a name is submitted but not approved, and further prayerful consideration is required. This should not put in question one's inspiration. It most likely confirms the worthiness on the part of the one being recommended. But circumstances known to the bishop or other priesthood leader may necessitate that you return to the process and seek further inspiration.

During the eight years I served as general Young Women president, I was blessed with five different counselors. With each change I felt a deep sense of loss. Should this raise a question of the inspiration involved in those original calls? Of course not. The counselors who were released were called to various other callings. Sister Elaine Jack was called as general Relief Society president; Sister Maurene Turley accompanied her husband, who was called as a mission president; Sister Pat Holland's family responsibilities increased as Elder Holland was at that time president of BYU and would shortly be called as a General Authority. The callings we have, for whatever period of time, help prepare us for what lies ahead. And with each new counselor, I benefited from her special gifts and talents and recognized her unique and important contribution.

Our Father in Heaven knows our strengths and weaknesses. He knows our feelings of inadequacy and our shortcomings, and yet he still calls us to our respective callings. It is important to have counselors who can compensate for those areas where we are less capable. The Lord knows our needs, and he knows the gifts and talents of others who might be called to assist. In a revelation given to Joseph Smith we read:

"Beware lest ye are deceived; and that ye may not be deceived seek ye earnestly the best gifts, always remembering for what they are given;

"For verily I say unto you, they are given for the benefit of those who love me and keep all my commandments, and him that seeketh so to do; that all may be benefited that seek or that ask of me. . . .

"And again, verily I say unto you, I would that ye should always remember, and always retain in your minds what those gifts are, that are given unto the church.

"For all have not every gift given unto them; for there are many gifts, and to every man is given a gift by the Spirit of God.

"To some is given one, and to some is given another, that all may be profited thereby" (D&C 46:8-12).

It has been my privilege to work with dedicated, inspired, and loyal counselors whose talents have allowed us together to reach heights that would never have been possible alone. As President Thomas S. Monson has stated: "Are our fellow workers by our side? Are we organized and working as a united team? Teamwork eliminates the weakness of a person standing alone and substitutes, the strength of workers serving together" (*New Era,* Young Women Special Issue, November 1985, p. 65).

THE ROLE OF COUNSELORS

The role of a counselor is to counsel. Counselors are an essential part of a presidency, bringing insights, experience, skills, and perceptions that magnify the capacity of the

president. One Relief Society president, expressing appreciation for her counselors, explained it this way: "I am strong on
vision. I have great ideas, but I don't have good landing gears.
I'm not as strong on details as I'd like to be. But with the help
of my counselors, we're able to fly successfully. I appreciate
their wise counsel and their support."

Effective counselors seek the Spirit of the Lord in knowing
their duty. They should strive to create a climate where the
Spirit is felt and thoughts and feelings are freely shared. They
listen to each other, avoid interrupting, and acknowledge the
role of the president in the responsibility for the final decisions.

One young sister relatively new in her leadership role as
president explained with some emotion that her counselor
refused to cooperate, refused to communicate with her, refused
to take counsel and accept decisions made by the president—
not once, not twice, but time after time. "She had wanted to be
president," was the explanation given for the conduct of this
troubled sister.

"Could something like this actually happen?" one might
ask. And the answer is yes, it could. The natural response to
solving a problem of this nature might simply be to release the
counselor, and in the minds of some, the sooner the better. It
would be called "firing" in some organizations. This might be a
"quick fix," but it is not the Lord's way. Only after an opportunity to seek understanding, to counsel together, and to encourage change would such action occur.

Counselors should never be offended when a decision is
different from the suggestion or recommendation that they
make. Every idea is worthwhile when it contributes to the
desired outcome. Decision making isn't the responsibility of the
counselors. This rests with the president after benefit of counsel. The counselors are then entrusted to support and sustain
the decision and to help in every way in its implementation.
However, there is great safety in the combined judgment of all
members of the presidency. If there is not unity in the
presidency concerning a matter, it is well to defer a final

decision, allowing for further deliberation and guidance of the Spirit.

Unity in a presidency does not mean that each one must think the same on every issue, and certainly not that the president come with plans already worked out, asking for support of her ideas. The spirit of unity allows for a free flow of expressions, some that may even be in opposition to each other. When ideas are given in a spirit of cooperation at the encouragement of the president, great insight can be gained. Realizing that these differences in opinion can be helpful and contribute to making wise decisions and recommendations, the presidency will strive to have an atmosphere of trust. President Brigham Young stated, "If we lack confidence in each other, and be jealous of each other, our peace will be destroyed. If we cultivate the principles of unshaken confidence in each other, our joy will be full" (*Discourses of Brigham Young,* comp. John A. Widtsoe [Salt Lake City: Deseret Book, 1954], p. 275).

There have been many times in my experience when the words of President George Q. Cannon, who was a counselor to Presidents Brigham Young, John Taylor, and Wilford Woodruff, have contributed to my commitment for unity. President Cannon said: "I suppose each one of us is fond of having his own way. I know I am. . . . But I do not like my own way well enough to want it in opposition to my brethren's way. That is our duty as the First Presidency of the Church. It is the duty of every presidency throughout the Church. . . . Suppose that one man has more wisdom than another; it is better to carry out a plan that is not so wise, if you are united on it. Speaking generally, a plan or policy that may be inferior in some respects is more effective if men are united upon it than a better plan would be upon which they were divided" (*Gospel Truth,* 2 vols. [Salt Lake City: Deseret Book, 1957], 1:207).

When members of a presidency pray with each other and for each other and for those they serve, they will be blessed beyond their natural abilities. They will feel a greater unity that will make them better able to serve.

Counselors represent and support the president in loyalty and spirit. Never have we had a more inspiring and powerful example of a loyal counselor than that of President Gordon B. Hinckley during the time he served as a counselor to Presidents Spencer W. Kimball, Ezra Taft Benson, and Howard W. Hunter. Never was there any hint of his assuming the responsibility of the president, even though in many instances because of their health he was carrying a major portion of the load. Yet always he acknowledged the president and his own role as counselor, and in every possible way was supportive. He was totally and completely trustworthy, never assuming a position that was not his. His example will be remembered as a magnificent lesson in the appropriate magnification of the role of a counselor. A counselor lifts the load of the president, however possible, and provides moral support and encouragement.

I remember many times, going into a meeting to make a presentation, when I felt concern for the responsibility that was mine. My counselors would kneel together with me in prayer. A feeling of love and support lifted my spirit and increased my confidence. After the meeting there was one counselor who would always whisper in my ear: "You are better than you realize." I never knew for sure what she meant by that, except that from the tone of her voice I felt her support and confidence.

It is not intended that a president shoulder the burden of leadership alone. We see the model of the presidency structure at all levels in every unit of the Church. Two counselors are called, first and second, each with specific areas of responsibility. Counselors assist and support the president in addressing problems, gathering information, making decisions, and carrying out programs.

It has been my experience that the contribution made by counselors is immeasurable. Besides helping to carry the heavy responsibilities of the president, they bring to a presidency different backgrounds and varied points of view. This added dimension contributes to wise decisions, leading to a much higher level of success in our efforts to build the kingdom.

CHAPTER TEN

SOLVING PROBLEMS AND CREATING UNITY

*And it came to pass that there was no contention
in the land, because of the love of God which
did dwell in the hearts of the people.*

4 NEPHI 1:15

The Salt Lake airport was unusually crowded one morning when, with ticket in hand, I maneuvered into the crowd moving in the direction I wanted to go. Just a few steps ahead of me was a young mother with a baby tucked securely under one arm and a heavy bag weighing her down on the other shoulder. I pushed forward, thinking I might be able to offer some assistance. When I got next to her, I observed her concern. Hidden down between the passengers were three little children, all hanging onto their mother's skirt, crowding against her legs and making it difficult for her to walk and maintain her balance in the crowd. She bent over in an effort to communicate with her little flock. By now I was within hearing distance, and between the loud announcements over the intercom, I heard this mother say in an anxious tone: "Listen to me. We must take hold of hands and hold on tight." At that very moment I felt a small hand slip into mine. I held it gently for a second or two and then it was quickly withdrawn. The child had responded—it was my hand that happened to be close and she took hold. For just a moment I felt an overwhelming sense of responsibility for this little child I didn't even know, and concern for a mother I had never met.

I wondered, what does it mean to take hold of hands and hold on tight? It means that in unity there is security. When we hold tight together, we can withstand the forces that might otherwise separate us. There is a power and a strength in unity that can overcome the risk of standing alone. When we are united in mind and heart, we can be a daunting force for good. In the April 1990 general conference, President Thomas S. Monson said: "Perhaps never in history has the need for cooperation, understanding and goodwill among all people—nations and individuals alike—been so urgent as today" (*Ensign*, May 1990, p. 5).

Unfortunately, our unity is often threatened by contention and other problems that arise. Leadership is seldom free from problems, which I prefer to call challenges. If you think there are no challenges, perhaps you aren't fully aware of the situation. Elder Neal A. Maxwell reminds us: "Imperfect people are, in fact, called by our perfect Lord to assist in His work" (*Ensign*, May 1982, p. 38). In our imperfections we will encounter the opportunity to learn how to cope with some degree of conflict. We will likely become acquainted with irritation, aggravation, exasperation, or at the least we will sometimes just be "miffed." It is to be hoped that we are not the cause of the problem, but that we can be a major influence in solving the problem. And in the possible event that we *are* the cause, may we have the sensitivity of spirit to turn to the Lord, who will show unto us our weakness so we will be humbled, and by the grace of God we will be made strong (see Ether 12:27).

We may not always be able to solve a problem immediately. It may take some time. But learning how to deal with the problem in an appropriate way should be a high priority for those called to lead. When we understand certain leadership principles and have the will and self-discipline to apply them, differences can usually be resolved. Elder Dallin H. Oaks writes: "The question is not *whether* we have such differences, but *how we manage them*" (*The Lord's Way* [Salt Lake City: Deseret Book, 1991], p. 200; italics in original). Leadership includes learning how to manage differences and avoid contention, criticism, and conflict as much as possible.

Contention and Conflict

Contention is sometimes referred to as "spiritual darkness." It is a tool of the adversary to "stir up the hearts of the people" (D&C 10:63). We read in Proverbs: "Only by pride cometh contention" (Proverbs 13:10). A warning comes from King Benjamin: "But, O my people, beware lest there shall arise contentions among you, and ye list to obey the evil spirit" (Mosiah 2:32). And in the words of the Lord himself to Nephi: "He that hath the spirit of contention is not of me, but is of the devil, who is the father of contention, and he stirreth up the hearts of men to contend with anger, one with another" (3 Nephi 11:29).

Conflict comes in many forms. Sometimes it is a simple disagreement over a decision being made. Sometimes it can become an argument over priorities or use of limited resources, or a feeling that things are unfair or unequal. Conflict may come from misunderstanding or competition or pride. Conflict is destructive to the Spirit.

Before looking elsewhere for the possible cause of contention or conflict, it is important to look within. The lyrics from the hymn "Truth Reflects upon Our Senses" (*Hymns*, no. 273) remind us of this principle:

> *Once I said unto another,*
> *"In thine eye there is a mote;*
> *If thou art a friend, a brother,*
> *Hold, and let me pull it out."*
> *But I could not see it fairly,*
> *For my sight was very dim.*
> *When I came to search more clearly,*
> *In mine eye there was a beam.*

We might all ask ourselves: Am I ever guilty of contributing to contention, conflict, or a lessening of the Spirit? Do I ever engage in any of the following?

- Looking to others as the source of the problem.
- Insisting on having my own way.

- Being impatient with the imperfections of others.
- Resisting change.
- Not understanding the principle of presidency and who is responsible for the final decision.
- Using authority inappropriately (unrighteous dominion).
- Finding fault.
- Gossiping, speaking ill of another.
- Being prideful, lacking humility.
- Feeling inadequate.
- Being unwilling to accept counsel (especially from someone less experienced).
- Being unwilling to admit error.
- Being unwilling to forgive and forget.
- Being unwilling to listen to others.
- Being competitive.
- Needing recognition.
- Feeling jealous.
- Resisting authority.
- Not understanding the order of the Church as a theocracy, not a democracy.
- Closing my heart to the whisperings of the Spirit.

When we honestly evaluate ourselves in these areas, we may not be able to solve a problem of contention and conflict, but we can correct, if needed, our response to the problem and thereby contribute to the solution.

RESOLVING CONTENTION AND CONFLICT

The first step in resolving contention and conflict is to determine the cause. Once the cause is identified, you can look for ways to resolve the problem. Be positive. Even in dealing with problems, many benefits can be realized when those involved become part of the solution: (1) new approaches might be considered, (2) underlying concerns can be brought forth and dealt with, (3) people are encouraged to clarify their views, and (4) better ideas can be produced with more creativity.

In resolving contention and conflict, no one should feel defeated or demeaned. Relationships should be maintained in a climate of trust and good will. Several types of responses can help maintain this atmosphere.

Accommodating means preserving and valuing a relationship ahead of personal preferences, assuming such an accommodation would not be in conflict with guiding principles.

Another approach is to *avoid confrontation*. When there seems little chance to resolve the conflict because of circumstances, if the issue isn't really critical, let it go.

Compromising makes sense when it is not related to fixed principles. There are standards that should not be compromised, but methods and practices and ideas are generally more open. Compromising is a means of working out a sharing situation in which all parties benefit.

Collaborating takes place when all the people involved in a decision accept and understand each other's goals and objectives and work together to achieve the best solution for all involved. This is clearly the ideal solution.

Contention and conflict should be avoided where possible, but when they occur they should not be feared. We should rather view them as something to be understood and handled in a positive way.

Years ago I saw a demonstration on "How to Disagree Agreeably" that left a lasting impression on my mind. Two people role-played a situation in which they were trying to resolve a major conflict, a difference of opinion. A large balloon was blown up as close to its full capacity as it could be filled without bursting. You might say it was blown "uptight." Every time a person offered a comment or question indicating a desire to understand before seeking to be understood, the moderator released a little air from the balloon, thus relieving some of the tension. Questions and statements that attacked the problem and not the person were most effective in releasing air: Help me understand. What is your recommendation? Is there something I am missing? What might be the consequence? Tell me how it seems to you.

Little by little, with every sincere question or comment, more air would escape. This process continued until all the air was expelled from the balloon and it was totally free from any pressure. It was no longer "uptight." When there is no pressure and no one is uptight—in other words, when you feel right toward each other—you can say anything. You can disagree agreeably. There can be differences of opinion without contention or conflict.

Confrontation often triggers a "fight or flight" response within. When we feel at peace and are filled with love, there is no fight and no flight. We are free from the desire to fight for our own way and be aggressive on one hand, or, on the other, to withdraw and abandon our responsibility.

In the writings of Paul we read: "Let all bitterness, and wrath, and anger, and clamour, and evil speaking, be put away from you" (Ephesians 4:31). He further admonishes us to set aside "all malice, and all guile, and hypocrisies, and envies, and all evil speakings" (1 Peter 2:1). Modern revelation instructs: "And see that there is no iniquity in the church, neither hardness with each other, neither lying, backbiting, nor evil speaking" (D&C 20:54); "Cease to find fault one with another" (D&C 88:124); and "Cease to speak evil one of another" (D&C 136:23).

All of those scriptures deal with speaking, or how we communicate with each other. Problem solving through communication is a skill that can be learned. Study the following matrix representing four communication styles and consider the effect of the language used in each quadrant.

	Punishing	Nonpunishing
Vague	1	2
Specific	3	4

Problem: The ball has been dropped on an assignment for a ward party.

Quadrant #1: Vague and Punishing

> Leader to individual: "You always question my decisions and want your own way."
>
> Possible response: "What's the problem? Why are you so upset with me?"
>
> Note: The person is being attacked and may not even know the reason. The problem is not solved and the relationship is threatened.

Quadrant #2: Vague and Nonpunishing

> Leader to individual: "Something is wrong. Things aren't working out."
>
> Possible response: "I wonder what is bothering her. What is she talking about? I'll just ignore it and maybe it will go away."
>
> Note: The problem is not solved, nor is the relationship endangered.

Quadrant #3: Specific and Punishing

Leader to individual: "When the decision was made about the ward party, you said you would be responsible for the music, and now as usual you are not supportive of the program. You've done nothing about it."

Possible response: "She doesn't understand. She doesn't care about me and it's her fault."

Note: Communicating the specific problem while attacking the individual may resolve the problem but in the process destroy a relationship, a person's confidence, and the spirit of cooperation.

Quadrant #4: Specific and Nonpunishing

Leader to individual: "I understand there has been no arrangement for the music for the ward party [state the problem specifically]. This will create a serious problem, since the music was to be the entire program [state the consequences]. Were you not aware of our understanding that you were to arrange for the music? [seek understanding]. What happened? Can I help you? [offer support]."

Possible response: "I did agree to be responsible for the program when it was decided that the Smith Family Singers would be a good possibility. I know them and was willing to contact them and make arrangements, but then I learned that they would be out of town on that evening. I tried to contact you several times but was unable to reach you. I didn't know what you wanted me to do, so I contacted Sister Brown. She said she thought you were aware of that and had taken care of it. I thought you had arranged for someone else."

Leader: "Obviously there has been some misunderstanding, some miscommunication. Let's talk about what we might do. Do you have any suggestions? How can I help you?"

Note: When the nonpunishing, specific approach is taken,

and listening with understanding takes place, communication is opened and problems can be addressed in a positive way. The leader does not fix blame or take away responsibility, leaving the person feeling like a failure. She addresses the problem in a specific, nonpunishing way, and problem solving through communication begins to take place.

Consider this same pattern when addressing problems within the family, where leadership skills are most important.

Problem: A mother is concerned by her daughter's messy, messy room.

Quadrant #1: Vague and Punishing

> Mom to daughter: "The way you keep your room is a disaster and a disgrace to our home."
> Possible response: "What is it about my room and about me that is so bad?"
> Note: This personal attack on the young woman does not solve the problem, and it puts the relationship at risk.

Quadrant #2: Vague and Nonpunishing

> Mom to daughter: "Our house is never tidy. I wish we could do something about it."
> Possible response: "What's bothering Mom today? Hopefully she'll get over it."
> Note: Daughter doesn't feel threatened but doesn't know what's causing the concern, and nothing is done to resolve the problem.

Quadrant #3: Specific and Punishing

> Mom to daughter: "The way you leave your clothes lying around is a disgrace. That potato-chip bag you threw in the corner of your room and all the other trash is inexcusable."
> Possible response: "I'm not good enough. My room is not

acceptable and my mom doesn't care or even understand. It's my room and she can stay out."

Note: The problem is not solved, and the relationship is aggravated if not destroyed.

Quadrant #4: Specific and Nonpunishing

Mom to daughter: "When I walked into your room I noticed your new skirt and sweater on the bench and your freshly ironed blouses lying on the bed. Also, an empty potato-chip bag was in the corner of your room [state the problem specifically]. When I saw this, I worried about your clothes being wrinkled when you want to wear them, and also about bugs that might be drawn to the potato-chip bag. This could become a bigger problem unless something is done [state the consequences]. Is this a problem I can help you with? [seek understanding and offer support]."

Possible response: "Well, I never have enough hangers for my blouses, and someone took my wastepaper basket that is usually in the corner."

Note: When we seek first to understand the situation by active listening, we are in a better position to resolve the problem. When our tone of voice and language convey a mood of understanding and not attacking, relationships can be maintained and even strengthened, rather than being lost over a problem that is far less important than those relationships. Negotiation can begin, and a discussion of how to fix the problem evolves.

Mother's response: "If I get you six hangers, will that be enough to ensure that your clothes will be hung up every day?"

Note: The negotiations continue, addressing the problem with the combined resources of those who care.

Don't Feed the Problem

President Gordon B. Hinckley has said: "A good leader starves the problems and feeds the opportunity. He doesn't let the problems get him down. We all have problems. We all have difficulties in our leadership, every one of us. We cannot let those become so much a part of our interests that we lose track of the bigger picture. Don't let the little problems worry you. . . . Oh, you have to deal with them, but deal with them and get them behind you" (From Port Harcourt, Nigeria, regional conference, priesthood leadership meeting, February 14, 1998).

Sometimes there seems to be no immediate solution to a problem. In those cases, we must avoid feeding the problem, keeping it alive by fueling the fire of disagreement. I had occasion to be talking with a very dedicated, recently called Relief Society president, Sister Smith (not her real name). Anxious to do everything right, she shared a concern, "a real problem," she said. She explained that there was a very sensitive situation she had to resolve, but her efforts had been in vain.

In a meeting it had been decided by the presidency (united in their opinion) that some printed materials would need to be prepared and put in a packet for a ward conference assignment. The secretary, who did not feel supportive of the decision and yet would be expected to take a major role in the preparation of the materials, expressed her strong objection. She further made it clear that she had no time to be involved in this project. The meeting closed.

The Relief Society president felt the need to get the job done even if she had to do it herself. She solicited the help of her counselors, and the work began moving forward. The secretary became aware that the project was going on without her, and without her having been notified. She was deeply offended. She felt left out and hurt.

The Relief Society president felt totally responsible for this problem and the offense she felt she had caused by the way she had handled the matter. She said she had visited the offended sister several times, had gone to her home and apologized, and was at a loss to know what she might do to repair the problem.

Is it possible that a leader's assuming the responsibility to "fix" every problem may actually be part of the problem? Sister Smith accepted the suggestion that, now that every effort had been made to resolve the concern, she let the secretary be responsible for her own feelings and quit assuming responsibility for a burden that was not hers. It was important that Sister Smith have a feeling of love and acceptance of this sister, and it was right for her to apologize if she had offended her. She could continue to keep contact and leave the door open for the secretary to be involved. But it was not right for her to be consumed and distracted from other duties and responsibilities by a problem that was not hers to solve at this point in time.

After about a week, Sister Smith shared with me her happy feelings and gratitude for her secretary. The sister who had been offended and felt left out in time came forth asking forgiveness for her lack of support and expressing her willingness to take over a major part of the work. When she was left to assume responsibility for her own feelings, she realized that she wanted to be involved.

In the process of problem solving, once proper acknowledgment and sincere apologies have been expressed for any misunderstanding, let it go. Do not feed the problem. Do not keep problems alive by rehashing and replaying matters that need to be forgotten. Close the door. Forgive and forget. There is great wisdom in the counsel of Brigham Young, "Avoid nursing the misunderstandings into difficulties" (*Discourses of Brigham Young,* comp. John A. Widtsoe [Salt Lake City: Deseret Book, 1975], p. 277).

It is a tool of the adversary to fuel the fire of contention, conflict, offense, and all other feelings that can lessen the Spirit and distract us from our work. As we seek to solve problems generated by contention, criticism, or conflict, let us remember the wise words of President Brigham Young: "When a difference of judgment exists between two parties, let them come together and lay their difficulties at each other's feet, laying themselves down in the cradle of humility, and say, 'Brother (or sister) I want to do right; yea, I will even wrong myself, to make you right.' Do you not think that a man or woman, acting in that manner towards his or her neighbor, would be justified by the law of righteousness?" (*Discourses of Brigham Young*, p. 276).

With this spirit of unity comes the desire and ability to set aside selfish interests, priorities, and personal preference for the good of the whole. It requires looking beyond ourselves and letting go of some things while reaching out and taking hands and holding tight to others.

My niece Shelly and I were sitting together in my living room visiting one day when her two-year-old son, Jake, burst in enthusiastically from the other room and began leaving evidence of his presence with fingerprints (and noseprints) all over the glass top of the coffee table. Shelly, somewhat concerned and feeling responsible for his proper behavior, responded quickly with clear instructions. "Oh, Jake," she said, "don't put your fingers on the glass." She didn't realize that I would want to save those fingerprints after he left. I came to Jake's rescue. "Don't worry about that, Shelly," I said emphatically. "It's okay." This happy two-year-old picked up on that saving communication quickly. To make sure the message got through, he reached out to his mom, put his hand on her cheek, and repeated with the same inflection, "Don't worry about it, Mom, it's okay."

I recognized immediately that there were at least three different points of view in this little encounter. Each of us had something different that we wanted to have happen. Jake wanted to look through the glass to see what was under the table. Shelly wanted her son to demonstrate proper behavior. I most wanted both mother and son to know how welcome they were regardless of anything else.

When we come to understand each other, there is a sense of unity that brings us together instead of dividing us. As leaders, if we are not clear in our purpose, knowing what it is we want to have happen, it is easy to become concerned or distracted—even discouraged—by some things that aren't really important, like fingerprints on the glass. And our Father in Heaven may want to touch our cheek gently and say, "Don't worry about that. It's okay." We must learn to let go of things that don't really matter and focus on coming together in purpose.

FOSTERING UNITY

When we as leaders in the Church are determined "in one mind and in one heart, united in all things," we shall be prepared to overtake the opposition (see 2 Nephi 1:21).

For many years at Church headquarters, the three women's auxiliaries of the Church—the Primary, Young Women, and Relief Society—were housed in different locations. The Relief Society had its offices in the beautiful building on the corner of North Temple and Main Street, the Relief Society Building, which had been built with funds donated by the Relief Society sisters throughout the world and had served this purpose for many years. In 1984, the Young Women and Primary organizations were located on different floors in the Church Office Building. Regular interaction between the organizations took place on quite a limited basis.

In 1986, a significant change occurred in the physical arrangements of these three organizations, thus providing greater opportunity for interaction and communication. At this time, Sister Barbara Winder had been called as the general Relief Society president. The idea of having two other organizations move into the Relief Society Building and take up the space that had traditionally been used by the Relief Society might have been a test for many. This was of little concern to Sister Winder. She had been prepared for this manner of thinking in her mind and heart for years. She and her husband lived on Winder Lane, where several Winder families lived close enough that, as she said, "the children would feel as welcome in one home as another." Resources were shared freely and they lived together in love and harmony. A special spirit of opening her heart and home was made ready from years of experience.

At this time the Relief Society Building needed to be refurbished with new carpets and wallcoverings and renovated to meet current building codes. During the renovation period, the Relief Society moved into the Church Office Building. Three organizations were housed on three floors in the same building. As the renovation and refurbishment of the historic Relief Society Building was nearing completion, an anticipation of our moving together was eminent.

The three presidents, Sister Winder of the Relief Society, Sister Dwan Young of the Primary, and I of the Young Women, together with our counselors and administrative assistants, attended the Salt Lake Temple. We were full of anticipation about coming together physically in the same building as well as drawing closer in heart and mind. After attending the temple we walked together over to the newly renovated building.

We stepped into the large and beautiful reception room of this historic setting. It was as if all those leaders from times past might have been united in lending their spirit and influence to this occasion. The room was carpeted from wall to wall, and in the center of the carpet was a large medallion pattern in exquisite colors, blending together the decor of the room, an artistic design drawing our attention to the center. We slipped our shoes off before walking on this newly laid carpet and stood in a circle at the edge of the design where we could admire it more closely.

In this spirit of excitement, anticipation, and delight, we spontaneously sat on the carpet around the center circle. From that experience we began to feel the power that we knew would come with the opportunity to work more closely together.

At this time, the Young Women organization was giving a lot of thought to values as a guide to making decisions and providing direction. The idea was suggested that the three organizations might consider adopting common values that would serve well during this moment in time when adjustments, accommodations, and flexibility would be required if we were to come together in unity. Each sister present felt a strong sense of loyalty to the organization for which she was responsible. After a considerable discussion involving different points of view, different needs, and some strong personal preferences, we created and adopted four values that we agreed would help us maintain a strong sense of unity under all circumstances.

The first value we agreed upon was *unity*. We would put the commitment to unity above any other preference. For example, even if we really would prefer placing a picture representing our organization in a more prominent, visible location than another, this would not erode the spirit of unity that must exist. If a person preferred one office over another because of a better view or convenience, opinions were freely expressed. But no office or physical arrangement offered any advantage that was more important than the advantage of unity.

The second value was *identity*. It would be essential that in our coming together we would not lessen the mission or uniqueness of each organization. For example, even though the name of the building would continue to be the Relief Society Building, the clear identity of all three organizations would be emphasized and represented in our new home.

The third value was *continuity*. Although each organization must maintain its individuality, we must lock arms, overlap, reach out in our planning, and provide, if it were possible, a bridge between each organization in an effort to avoid losing even one member in transition from one organization to another. Our loyalty would bridge the gaps. For example, we would be more knowledgeable of the goals and aims of each organization.

And finally, the fourth value was *equity*. This did not mean that everyone would have or need the same things, but that whatever was available could be shared by all. This proved to be a tremendous advantage in some cases. For example, when we all shared what was in our cupboards to be used on the occasion of a little luncheon, we now each had the full range of resources from paper plates to fine china. But I can tell you there was much more in this coming together than sharing dishes.

Christmastime seemed like a great occasion to demonstrate this wonderful feeling of uniting on the basis of these four values. Christmas trees of three different sizes, large, medium, and smaller, were placed side by side in the large reception room (Unity). Each tree had ornaments representative of the organization it stood for (Identity). Each tree was as elegant as the other (Equity), and the placement of the trees was such that there was just a slight overlapping of the branches of one tree reaching out and touching the one next to it (Continuity). We didn't assume that people who visited the building necessarily caught the message of the three trees, but we did. And when Christmas was over and the trees representing the values that would bind us together were removed, the bonds of love and unity remained.

The powerful impact of such unity is observed throughout the Church. I have attended many Young Women conferences where the services of the Relief Society sisters have been an obvious blessing. I am aware of Young Women activities that have involved making things to be used in the nursery and Primary. And whether a sister serves in Primary, Young Women, or Relief Society, there is indeed a coming together and participation in Relief Society events where the bridge from one organization to the next is felt. This support for each other is very significant, since the order of the Church is such that the organization we are helping at this time may very well be the one we will be called to serve in next month or next year.

I remember one occasion when a meeting was being held to resolve some major differences between two groups. And although the perspective of each was right from their vantage point, there would have to be a coming together before moving forward. The priesthood leader who was conducting the meeting began with a rather lengthy explanation of the need to come together in unity. This important instruction was given even before the prayer was offered. The prayer then offered was specific in its request for a spirit of unity while the matters at hand were being discussed. There was a feeling of peace and quiet in the room. We felt the presence of the Spirit. We were ready to begin. The priesthood leader then offered this request: "If at any time during our discussion, any one of you feels a lessening of the Spirit, please make it known and we will stop and invoke the Spirit of the Lord in prayer once again."

This was for me an unusual experience. I felt the personal responsibility to feel the Spirit, listen to the Spirit, and follow. This meeting provided an opportunity to express weighty matters. Each person's comments suggested a sincere desire to come together. This desire should be in our hearts in every meeting, so that our contributions, whether in words or just in our presence, add to the feeling of having our hearts knit together in love.

There is so much at stake as we face the future with its ever-increasing opposition. May it be recorded that the women in the Church in our time and season were united and followed the admonition of President Gordon B. Hinckley: "Unitedly, working hand in hand, we shall move forward as servants of the living God, doing the work of His Beloved Son, our Master, whom we serve and whose name we seek to glorify" (*Ensign*, May 1995, p. 71).

PART THREE

THE SPIRIT
OF
LEADERSHIP

CHAPTER ELEVEN

WHERE DO I FIND MY STRENGTH?

I know that I am nothing; as to my strength I am weak;
therefore I will not boast of myself, but I will boast
of my God, for in his strength I can do all things.
ALMA 26:12

Do you remember a time when you might have been asked for a résumé, a transcript, or a letter of recommendation that would have a significant bearing on your opportunity to be accepted to a college, a company, or a position of leadership? In a résumé we list our strengths, our accomplishments, our experience, and any other evidence that our wisdom, our gifts and talents, our personality, our skills and attributes, and our dedication should edge out others who may be competing for the opening. And if we do edge out others and get the job, is there a sense of pride in our victory?

The Lord's way is not man's way. We do not submit a résumé or even a letter of recommendation for a call to leadership in the Church. We never apply, and when interviewed we may immediately feel encompassed about by reminders of our lack of qualifications, our weaknesses, and our limitations. There may be many who seem much more qualified, and yet we "get the job."

Without an impressive résumé as evidence of our qualification, where do we turn for help in this major responsibility? When we accept a calling to be a leader in the Church, a door is opened to strength, power, and influence that we do not have on our own.

When my husband was called to preside over the Canada Vancouver Mission, a friend with some experience shared a story that had an element of truth in it—at least for me, if not for Heber. As the story goes, a new mission president's first response is an earnest desire to be the best mission president the Church has ever had. A few weeks into his calling he catches a glimpse of reality, and his desire is adjusted somewhat, to be just *one* of the best mission presidents the Church has ever had. In time his desire has nothing to do with the comparison with other mission presidents; he just wants to do the best he can. The story ends there, but I would add the following sequel that in time must become a reality if we are to accomplish the work given us to do. I suggest that our desire should not be to do better than someone else, or even to do the best we can do, but rather should expand to include what can be accomplished in the strength of the Lord. That goes far beyond the best we can do by ourselves.

In his famous poem "Invictus," author William Ernest Henley may be admirable in dedication and confidence, but he is woefully lacking in his understanding of his source of strength. The last verse of this poem, addressing challenges of every kind, ends with these words:

> *It matters not how strait the gate,*
> *How charged with punishments the scroll,*
> *I am the master of my fate;*
> *I am the captain of my soul.*
>
> (101 Famous Poems [New York: Reilly
> & Lee, 1958], p. 95)

This poet will yet learn that he is neither the master of his fate nor the captain of his soul. In the words of King Benjamin, "I say unto you that if ye should serve him who has created you from the beginning, and is preserving you from day to day, by lending you breath, that ye may live and move and do according to your own will, and even supporting you from one moment to another—I say, if ye should serve him with all your whole souls yet ye would be unprofitable servants" (Mosiah 2:21).

THE QUEST FOR PREPARATION

With every new calling, we seek for instant qualifications to compensate for our limitations. As one of my friends explained at the time of a calling, "I want to learn as fast as I can before people find out what I don't know." Along the way, we will have ample opportunity to be stripped of pride.

This acknowledgment of our own inadequacies is an important part of our preparing to receive the strength that is available to us. Our kind Father in Heaven provides a curriculum customized for our individual growth. He promises: "And if men come unto me I will show unto them their weakness. I give unto men weakness that they may be humble; and my grace is sufficient for all men that humble themselves before me; for if they humble themselves before me, and have faith in me, then will I make weak things become strong unto them" (Ether 12:27).

Our first step in gaining access to this strength is as simple as desire. We should desire, not to outshine someone else with our gifts and talents, but rather to have access to the strength of the Lord that will lift us up beyond our natural ability. When we know that on our own we can do nothing of any consequence, then we are ready to receive.

Elder Neal A. Maxwell asks: "Is there not deep humility in the majestic Miracle Worker who acknowledged, 'I can of my own self do nothing'? (John 5:30.) Jesus never misused or doubted His power, but He was never confused about its Source either. But we mortals, even when otherwise modest, often are willing to display our accumulated accomplishments as if we had done them all by ourselves" (*Meek and Lowly* [Salt Lake City: Deseret Book, 1987], p. 9).

Part of our weakness is that we are mortal, in a fallen state. We are surrounded by the reality of mortality and our limited ability. We draw upon the Lord when we yield to the enticings of the Holy Spirit and become as saints through the atonement of Christ the Lord. We become childlike, submissive, meek,

121

humble, full of love, willing to submit to all things our Father in Heaven requires of us (see Mosiah 3:19).

Thus we are lifted up far beyond our natural ability. We realize that even our painful limitations and infirmities can be a blessing to us. Consider the insight Paul gained as he faced his leadership challenges: "And lest I should be exalted above measure through the abundance of the revelations, there was given to me a thorn in the flesh, the messenger of Satan to buffet me, lest I should be exalted above measure. For this thing I besought the Lord thrice, that it might depart from me. And he said unto me, My grace is sufficient for thee: for my strength is made perfect in weakness. Most gladly therefore will I rather glory in my infirmities, that the power of Christ may rest upon me. Therefore I take pleasure in infirmities, in reproaches, . . . for Christ's sake: for when I am weak, then am I strong" (2 Corinthians 12:7–10).

THE INVITATION AND PROMISE

In the chapel of the Bountiful Temple, just behind and above the pulpit is the familiar picture of the resurrected Lord with arms outstretched, signifying that comforting, reassuring message and invitation, "Come unto me." That invitation is current, immediate, and always present.

One early morning as I sat on the back row in the chapel, waiting to take my place as an ordinance worker, I looked at the open arms of the Savior and considered the invitation that drew me in. At the organ was an elderly, white-haired brother, and the strains of the music "More Holiness Give Me" (*Hymns,* no. 131) filled the room, while a yearning filled my heart.

More purity give me,
More strength to o'ercome,
More freedom from earthstains,
More longing for home.
More fit for the kingdom,
More used would I be,
More blessed and holy–
More, Savior, like thee.

In that quiet moment of solitude, while I was reaching for more, I looked again at the open arms of our Savior and into my heart and mind came the words, "All that I have is yours. Can there be more?" With the invitation, "Come unto me," is a promise of everything else. All that he has is ours.

The scriptures provide a long list of promises, and they go on to record remarkable events giving evidence that those promises are sure. A pattern emerges. Note that the invitation "Draw near unto me" is followed by a promise, "And I will draw near unto you." Another invitation, "Seek me diligently," is followed by another promise, "And ye shall find me." The pattern continues, "Ask, and ye shall receive; knock, and it shall be opened unto you" (D&C 88:63). We find our strength in our willingness to accept his invitation.

The strength given is exactly what is needed for the circumstance. Helaman wrote of his two thousand stripling warriors who fought the Lamanites with such courage: "They had fought as if with the strength of God; yea, never were men known to have fought with such miraculous strength" (Alma 56:56). Keep in mind that these were young men without experience. They never had fought before (see Alma 56:47). This was not a call or an assignment they were familiar with. Yet they were successful because the Lord was with them.

David was only a youth when he went before Goliath. He knew the source of his strength. Speaking to Saul, this young man declared with confidence: "The Lord that delivered me out of the paw of the lion, and out of the paw of the bear, he will deliver me out of the hand of this Philistine." Approaching Goliath, he compared the resources of the giant with his own: "Thou comest to me with a sword, and with a spear, and with a shield: but I come to thee in the name of the Lord of hosts, the God of the armies of Israel, whom thou hast defied. This day will the Lord deliver thee into mine hand" (1 Samuel 17:37, 45-46).

The strength of the Lord is available not only in our major battles against the enemy but also in our private battles against weaknesses and infirmities. His grace, this "divine means of help or strength, given through the bounteous mercy and love of Jesus Christ," is an enabling power we can call upon when we have expended our own best efforts (see Bible Dictionary, p. 697). This compensation for our weaknesses does not come at the end of life or even the end of the day, but at the end of our own best efforts.

Throughout my life I have been plagued, frustrated, and humbled by a severe lack of a physical sense of direction. It is so extreme that reading a map and finding my way to a speaking engagement is far more stressful to me than delivering the speech upon arrival. I'm somewhat comforted in the fact that my two sisters suffer the same problem. My sister Shirley explains gratefully, "I don't know east from west, north from south, or up from down, but I do know right from wrong." Maybe that's enough, when we know where to turn for further direction.

I have finally acknowledged that this is one of my handicaps, "a thorn in the flesh," an embarrassment, to say the least. But it need not be. In earnest prayer I always leave home with a plea, "Father, lead me, guide me, walk beside me, help me find the way." To some this may seem a trivial matter, but for me it is not.

I have in my journal many, many accounts of times when I have pulled off the highway to try to get my bearings, only to have someone out mowing the lawn, walking a dog, or doing whatever activity would place them at the spot where I needed direction. In one case where the address was incomplete, the map was complicated (they all are for me), and time was running out, a stranger going the opposite direction rolled down his car window to offer help. I explained my difficulty and he called out, "Follow me." He turned his car around, drove to the entrance of the church parking lot, honked, pointed, waved, and drove on.

I share this illustration as evidence that when we are in the Lord's service, he will make up for our limitations. When self-reliance and self-confidence give way, our struggles open the door to a deeper understanding of Christ's condescension and his commitment to succor us, bless us, comfort us, and even pray for us. He is our advocate with the Father.

Surely he is the good shepherd who pleads our cause and adds to our meager offering all that is needed. Consider the lines from Harry Rowe Shelley's "The King of Love My Shepherd Is":

> The King of Love my Shepherd is
> Whose goodness faileth never.
> I nothing lack if I am his
> And he is mine forever.
> Perverse and foolish oft I strayed,
> But yet in love he sought me,
> And on his shoulder gently laid
> And home rejoicing brought me.

He will lift us up, and with his help our performance will be not only acceptable but remarkable.

Our Source of Strength

The first step when we receive a call to lead is not to prepare a résumé of our abilities but rather to acknowledge our inabilities. It is possible that we will enjoy many expressions of commendation and even notes of praise. If this happens, may we be humble enough to acknowledge our own nothingness and give thanks to the Lord. A great example is given us by Ammon, who enjoyed such great missionary success among the Lamanites. Can't you imagine a missionary's urge to tell everyone of such success? Wouldn't it be natural to write home and have it announced in the ward or, even better, in stake conference? But listen to the words of Ammon: "I do not boast in my own strength, nor in my own wisdom; but behold, my joy is full, yea, my heart is brim with joy, and I will rejoice in my God. Yea, I know that I am nothing; as to my strength I am weak; therefore I will not boast of myself, but I will boast of my God, for in his strength I can do all things; yea, behold, many mighty miracles we have wrought in this land, for which we will praise his name forever" (Alma 26:11–12).

We do not glory in ourselves, but in our Lord. And when we serve without words of commendation or appreciation, even when such approval seems deserved, we remember the Master whom we serve, knowing it is his commendation that we seek.

One summer I attended a three-day youth survival camp where we were all expected to rappel over the edge of a mountain that dropped eighty feet to the canyon floor below. Many of the eager youth, mostly the boys, lined up willingly to take their turns. Everyone stood with attention riveted on Brother Tolman, the instructor. He began explaining the dangers, the need to follow directions, and finally, the essential nature of how to use the rope to move from the top of the mountain to the destination below.

When it came to my turn, I asked for one more review of the instructions that had already been given. I wanted to hear all of them, what to do and what not to do. The ground below was not visible from the top of the mountain, which added to the uncertainty of stepping off the ledge with only the rope to hang on to. Hanging over the edge of the mountain, I was able to plant my feet firmly against the solid rock with my body almost perpendicular to the wall in front of me. Slowly I inched my way down the mountain, listening for the reassurance of Brother Tolman's instructions from the top, even though I couldn't see him.

About halfway down, forty feet from the top and forty feet from the bottom, I paused and looked down. Taking a deep breath, I changed my perspective by looking up. It was then that I sensed the significance of the rope, the strength of the rope, the essential nature of the rope, my dependence upon the rope if I was to survive this experience. On my own I could neither climb back up nor ease myself to the surface below. Without the rope I could do nothing.

In a mistaken display of self-reliance and self-confidence, I could let go of the rope if I chose to, at least with one hand. It would be there whether I chose to hang on tight or not. The strength of the rope, my lifeline to safety, was never in question.

I have come to think of that rope as being like our life-saving covenants. It is in the ordinances and the covenants that are available to us only in the gospel of Jesus Christ that we are bound to him, that his strength is made available to us. If we hold tight, we shall reach our destination.

President George Q. Cannon explains this relationship: "When we went forth into the waters of baptism and covenanted with our Father in heaven to serve Him and keep His commandments, He bound Himself also by covenant to us, that He would never desert us, never leave us to ourselves, never forget us, that in the midst of trials and hardships, when everything was arrayed against us, He would be near unto us and would sustain us. That was His covenant, and He has amply fulfilled it up to the present time and has shown that we can tie to the promises that He has made. We have proved these things through experience" (*Gospel Truth,* 2 vols. [Salt Lake City: Deseret Book, 1957], 1:134).

He assures us that he is the rope and the hope, the rod of iron and the gentle master teacher who calls encouragement from above. Like Nephi, we understand where to turn for strength: "O Lord, I have trusted in thee, and I will trust in thee forever. I will not put my trust in the arm of flesh; for I know that cursed is he that putteth his trust in the arm of flesh. Yea, cursed is he that putteth his trust in man or maketh flesh his arm" (2 Nephi 4:34).

At the BYU/Relief Society Women's Conference in 1998, Virginia Pearce reminded us: "Success is an affliction to our soul unless we recognize the source of strength." The Nephite dissenters and the Lamanites learned something of how strength can be lost as they tried to overcome their challenges and fight their battles: "And because of this their . . . boastings in their own strength, they were left in their own strength; therefore they did not prosper, but were afflicted and smitten, and driven before the Lamanites, until they had lost possession of almost all their lands" (Helaman 4:13).

OUR STEWARDSHIP FOR THE STRENGTH WE ARE GIVEN

Christ instructs: "Heal the sick, cleanse the lepers, raise the dead, cast out devils: freely ye have received, freely give" (Matthew 10:8). As we travel through life, we will encounter others who need to be lifted, encouraged, and sustained. In the New Testament, we learn how the strength we are given can bless those on our path. The book of Acts tells of a man who was carried daily to the gates of the temple to ask alms of those who entered. As Peter and John approached the temple, the man "asked an alms. And Peter, fastening his eyes upon him with John, said, Look on us. And he gave heed unto them, expecting to receive something of them. Then Peter said, Silver and gold have I none; but such as I have give I thee: In the name of Jesus Christ of Nazareth rise up and walk. And he took him by the right hand, and lifted him up: and immediately his feet and ankle bones received strength" (Acts 3:3–7).

Peter did his part: He reached out and took the one in need by the hand. And then the power given him by Jesus Christ blessed the one in need. Peter called upon the power of the Lord through the authority of the priesthood, but all of us can draw strength from the blessings poured out by the Master.

A few years ago I received a letter written by a thirteen-year-old girl, a patient in the Primary Children's Hospital. She had heard of a family who were suffering grave concern over one of their children, and had penned this letter:

"Dear Brother and Sister Doxey:

"How is your family doing? My name is Erica Monson. I am from Ely, Nevada. I am in Primary Children's Hospital. I'm getting better. I know how hard things are for you and your family, even though I'm thirteen. I hope that your daughter Kristen is lucky and finds the right donor so she can hopefully live to be a young woman. If I was old enough to donate and wasn't on medication for my liver, I would see if I matched your daughter's type. If I could I would do everything to make it so she would be able to live. I hope and pray for the best for your family.

"Love, Erica Monson

"P.S. If there is anything I can do, please feel free to write to me."

The message of this letter bears witness of her faith. The offer to give of herself to save another is evidence of the source of her strength, a source she clearly recognizes even at her young age.

As covenant children of our Father in heaven, we are as entitled to receive his strength as all those who have kept the covenants and gone before us. I am deeply impressed by the last twenty years of Moroni's life. He was alone. All of his friends and family had been killed. He had to hide himself from his enemies. He was always on the move, trying to find his own shelter, trying to sustain himself physically, and all the while keeping secure the sacred records his father had entrusted to him. He was a mortal like you and me, but during all those long years of trial and loneliness he was sustained by the same promises we hear each week in the sacramental prayer: He always remembered Christ; he kept His commandments and he had His spirit to be with him. Finally, Moroni was able to express his remarkable testimony and warning. He was able to figuratively look each of us in the eye and say, "I exhort you to remember" (Moroni 10:27).

When we remember the source of our strength, we as leaders can lead, guide, and walk beside others, accepting the invitation to come unto Christ, knowing that his promises are sure. In our leadership responsibilities and in our personal lives, may the words of Ammon fill our hearts with humility and great faith: "Yea, I know that I am nothing; as to my strength I am weak; therefore I will not boast of myself, but I will boast of my God, for in his strength I can do all things" (Alma 26:12).

CHAPTER TWELVE

GUIDED BY THE SPIRIT

Behold, I will tell you in your mind and in your heart,
by the Holy Ghost, which shall come upon you
and which shall dwell in your heart.

D & C 8:2

Faithful leaders in the Church are blessed with capacity that extends beyond their natural ability, beyond logic and reason, beyond experience and maturity. We believe in personal revelation relating to our area of responsibility and stewardship. The Holy Ghost is a gift from God, like a private tutor according to God's wisdom and our worthiness. Each of us can have the whisperings of the Spirit in our heart and soul as we seek to lead, guide, and walk beside those with whom we labor for a time.

When led by the Spirit in our callings, we learn things we didn't know on our own. Consider, for example, the theme young women are repeating worldwide in many languages as they speak of making and keeping sacred covenants and preparing to receive the ordinances of the temple. Could that theme have sprung from some academic study of teenage growth and young girls' social needs? We know that things of that nature come through the promptings of the Holy Spirit after much preparation. Vision and revelation come by the power of the Holy Ghost, which is bestowed on *all* members of the Church through the laying on of hands. As the Lord declared, "On my servants and on my handmaidens I will pour out in those days of my Spirit; and they shall prophesy" (Acts 2:18).

Elder Bruce R. McConkie explains: "I as an individual and you as an individual can come to know the things of God by the power of the Spirit. One thing the Lord said was, ' . . . I will tell you in your mind and in your heart, by the Holy Ghost, which shall come upon you and which shall dwell in your heart. Now, behold, this is the spirit of revelation' (D&C 8:2-3).

"This revelation speaks of spirit speaking to spirit, the Holy Spirit speaking to the spirit within me and in a way incomprehensible to the mind, but plain and clear to spiritual understanding, conveying knowledge, giving intelligence, giving truth and giving sure knowledge of the things of God" ("How to Get Personal Revelation," BYU Devotional Address, October 11, 1966, p. 5).

This knowledge that comes from the Spirit is not limited to age and experience, but rather is predicated on worthiness and willingness to seek.

RECOGNIZING THE SPIRIT

The Prophet Joseph Smith spoke about the spirit of revelation and how it might be recognized: "A person may profit by noticing the first intimation of the spirit of revelation; for instance, when you feel pure intelligence flowing into you, it may give you sudden strokes of ideas . . . and thus by learning the Spirit of God and understanding it, you may grow into the principle of revelation, until you become perfect in Christ Jesus" (*Teachings of the Prophet Joseph Smith,* comp. Joseph Fielding Smith [Salt Lake City: Deseret Book, 1977], p. 151).

The voice of the Spirit speaks to the mind and heart. Although it is referred to as a *voice,* it comes usually as a *feeling.* In the Book of Mormon we read about how Laman and Lemuel lost the Spirit when they rebelled against the Lord. Their brother Nephi rebuked them, saying, "Ye have heard his voice from time to time; and he hath spoken unto you in a still small voice, but ye were *past feeling,* that ye could not *feel* his words" (1 Nephi 17:45; italics added).

Our conscience responds to the whisperings and guidance of the Holy Ghost and influences our mind and heart. In an *Ensign* article years ago, Elder John H. Groberg offered the following list, modified from a seminary outline, suggesting how to discern when you have the Spirit. This attracted my interest and has continued to be a reference for me in times of self-evaluation.

WHEN YOU HAVE THE SPIRIT	WHEN YOU DO NOT HAVE THE SPIRIT
1. You generally feel happy and calm.	1. You may feel unhappy, depressed, confused, frustrated most of the time.
2. You feel full of light.	2. You may feel heavy, full of darkness.
3. Your mind is clear.	3. Your mind may be muddled.
4. You feel love for the Lord and others.	4. You may feel empty, hollow, cold inside.
5. You feel generous.	5. You may feel selfish, possessive, self-centered.
6. Nobody can offend you.	6. You may be offended easily.
7. You are very forgiving and kind.	7. You may usually be on the defensive.
8. You feel confident in what you do.	8. You may become discouraged easily.
9. You don't mind others seeing what you are doing.	9. You may become secretive, evasive.
10. You want to be with those who love you—especially family members.	10. You may want to be alone most of the time. You avoid others—especially family members.
11. You are glad when others succeed.	11. You may be envious almost constantly of what others do and what they have.

12. You want to help others be happy, even those opposed to you.	12. You may want to get even and show others up.
13. You willingly perform Church work.	13. You may feel hesitant, unworthy, and unwilling to perform Church ordinances.
14. You feel like praying and reading the scriptures.	14. You may not want to pray or read scriptures.
15. You wish you could keep all the Lord's commandments.	15. You may find the commandments of God and rules of the family bothersome, restricting, or senseless.
16. You usually control your appetites and emotions. You are calm and control your speech; you feel no anger.	16. You may be a slave to your appetites. You give way to strong anger and outspokenness.
17. You generally feel a deep desire to help others— usually in a way no one else will know about.	17. When you help others, your main desire may be to have your actions noticed.
18. You speak and think good about others.	18. You are critical of others, especially family members and those in authority.
19. You feel sorrow when others have problems and sincerely desire to help them.	19. You may often question others' motives and secretly delight in their problems.
20. You realize that your thoughts and your actions are open to God.	20. You may feel that what you do and think is only your business and no one else knows or cares.

(*Ensign,* April 1986, pp. 70-71)

How Do We Achieve Spirituality?

President Boyd K. Packer teaches: "The Spirit does not get our attention by shouting or shaking us with a heavy hand. Rather it whispers. It caresses so gently that if we are preoccupied we may not feel it at all. . . . Occasionally it will press just firmly enough for us to pay heed. But most of the time, if we do not heed the gentle feeling, the Spirit will withdraw and wait until we come seeking" (*Ensign,* January 1983, p. 53).

Elder Dallin H. Oaks has written: "How do we achieve spirituality? How do we attain that degree of holiness wherein we can have the constant companionship of the Holy Ghost and view and evaluate the things of this world with a perspective of eternity?

"We seek spirituality through faith, repentance, and baptism; through forgiveness of one another; through fasting and prayer; through righteous desires and pure thoughts and actions. We seek spirituality through service to our fellowmen; through worship; through feasting on the word of God, in the scriptures and in the teachings of the living prophets. We attain spirituality through making and keeping covenants with the Lord, through conscientiously trying to keep all the commandments of God. Spirituality is not acquired suddenly. It is the consequence of a succession of right choices. It is the harvest of a righteous life" (*Pure in Heart* [Salt Lake City: Bookcraft, 1988], p. 123).

Our level of spirituality determines our readiness to receive revelation. Elder Bruce R. McConkie asks: "Would you like a formula to tell you how to get personal revelation? It might be written in many ways. My formula is simply this:

"1. Search the Scriptures.

"2. Keep the Commandments.

"3. Ask in Faith" (*"How to Get Personal Revelation,"* p. 8).

I testify that this formula works. I have tested it over and over again. One occasion that will remain forever in my mind occurred following general conference, April 7, 1984. I had been called as the Young Women general president of the Church. At that time both President Spencer W. Kimball and President Marion G. Romney of the First Presidency were ill. President Gordon B. Hinckley was carrying a heavy load, and there was much to be done. It was not until six weeks later that counselors were called and set apart to the Young Women general presidency.

Without the benefit, wisdom, experience, support, and insight of counselors, I felt the weight of responsibility resting heavily on my shoulders. I felt alone. The words of Nephi came to my mind from my study of the scriptures, "If God had commanded me to do all things I could do them" (1 Nephi 17:50). I felt further direction when I read, "And I, Nephi, did go into the mount oft, and I did pray oft unto the Lord; wherefore the Lord showed unto me great things" (1 Nephi 18:3). I wanted to know the Lord's will and I wanted to carry it out. I knew that if I could be blessed with a sense of direction—knowing what the Lord wanted to have happen—there were many who would be called to assist. I knew, as we all do, that the Lord's will for his children is for us to understand the ordinances and covenants that bring us unto Christ. But I didn't know specifically what needed to be put in place for the young women in this particular time in the history of the Church to help accelerate their preparation. I searched the scriptures. I tried to keep the commandments. I asked in faith and tried to listen patiently for the answer. After many prayers, I heard in my mind and my heart, "Be of good cheer, for I will lead you along" (D&C 78:18). And another answer came to another fervent prayer, "Be thou humble; and the Lord thy God shall lead thee by the hand, and give thee answer to thy prayers" (D&C 112:10). That was answer enough for the time being, and with it came an assurance that more would come as needed.

At the dedication of the Relief Society monument to women in Nauvoo in 1978, I heard Elder Bruce R. McConkie quote Alma 32:23, which states that the Lord "imparteth his word by angels unto men, yea, not only men but women also."

He then said: "Where spiritual things are concerned, as pertaining to all of the gifts of the Spirit, with reference to the receipt of revelation, the gaining of testimonies, and the seeing of visions, in all matters that pertain to godliness and holiness and which are brought to pass as a result of personal righteousness—in all these things men and women stand in a position of absolute equality before the Lord. He is no respecter of persons nor of sexes . . . and he delights to honor those who serve him in righteousness unto the end—both male and female. It is to them that he promises to reveal all the hidden mysteries of his kingdom" (*Ensign,* January 1979, p. 61).

It is in asking that we receive, and in knocking that the door is opened to us. Our Father in heaven is anxious for us as leaders to inquire thoughtfully, prayerfully, and faithfully, and to expect to hear the promptings of the Spirit in answer to our earnest supplication.

KEEPING THE SPIRIT

As leaders, we have as our constant aim a desire to keep the Spirit with us. But in a world full of turmoil and the tendencies of the "natural man" (see Mosiah 3:19), it requires diligence to be a true disciple and a worthy leader. We read in the scriptures of the ten virgins, five who had oil in their lamps and five who did not (see Matthew 25:1-13). As women leaders, we must have our lamps filled with oil. President Harold B. Lee explains: "The Lord gives us, each one, a lamp to carry, but whether or not we shall have oil in our lamps depends solely on each one of us. Whether or not we keep the commandments and supply the needed oil to light our way and to guide us on our way depends upon each of us individually. We cannot borrow from our Church membership. We cannot borrow from an illustrious ancestry. Whether or not we have oil in our lamps, I repeat, depends solely upon each one of us, and it is determined by our faithfulness in keeping the commandments of the living God" (Conference Report, October 1951, p. 30).

It behooves all of us to strive to do those things that

increase our receptivity to the whisperings of the Spirit through diligence and obedience. Even the prophets seek this great advantage. At the close of general conference in 1975, President Kimball told the congregation: "While sitting here, I have made up my mind that when I go home from this conference this night there are many, many areas of my life that I can perfect. I have made a mental list of them, and I expect to go to work as soon as we get through with conference" (*Ensign,* November 1975, p. 111).

Surely this example is one of diligence. When there seems to be a lessening of the Spirit, the work cannot proceed with the same effectiveness. We are more easily delayed, distracted, and discouraged. Having the Spirit in our lives is essential to doing the Lord's work the Lord's way.

Much of the weight of leadership lies in the responsibility of the leader to make right decisions. How, then, do we make decisions directed by the Spirit? Elder Marvin J. Ashton often said, "Information leads to inspiration." And I would add, "Inspiration leads to wise decisions."

Here are some elements of wise decision making:

1. When decisions are being made, major or minor, focus on what it is you want to have happen. Weigh decisions by asking, "Will this decision move toward or away from the ultimate goal of bringing souls unto Christ?"

2. Gather all the information you can. Start by learning from the scriptures. The Lord instructs: "You must study it out in your mind; then you must ask me if it be right, and if it is right I will cause that your bosom shall burn within you; therefore, you shall feel that it is right. But if it be not right you shall have no such feelings, but you shall have a stupor of thought that shall cause you to forget the thing which is wrong" (D&C 9:8-9). Continue learning by counseling with others.

3. Pray. As a leader with weighty responsibilities, consider the comfort and blessing of this invitation from our Father: "Draw near unto me and I will draw near unto you; seek me diligently and ye shall find me; ask, and ye shall receive; knock,

and it shall be opened unto you. Whatsoever ye ask the Father in my name it shall be given unto you, that is expedient for you" (D&C 88:63–64).

And what can we talk to our Father in heaven about? What manner of questions might be appropriate? What problems might we seek help for? I'm convinced that if there is anything that matters to us, it matters to our Father in heaven, and he will hear our earnest plea. To reassure us that no aspect of our work is of little consequence, we read from Alma 37:36–37: "Yea, and cry unto God for all thy support; yea, let all thy doings be unto the Lord, and whithersoever thou goest let it be in the Lord; yea, let all thy thoughts be directed unto the Lord; yea, let the affections of thy heart be placed upon the Lord forever."

And if that isn't enough to encompass all the questions or concerns that we might have, the counsel continues: "Counsel with the Lord in all thy doings, and he will direct thee for good; yea, when thou liest down at night lie down unto the Lord, that he may watch over you in your sleep; and when thou risest in the morning let thy heart be full of thanks unto God; and if ye do these things, ye shall be lifted up at the last day."

Is there anything that we cannot inquire of the Lord? I think not. It is the leader's responsibility to formulate the questions, to study things out, asking what to plan, whom to call, how to deal with a problem, how to gain support, how to make preparation, how to manage the budget, how to counsel, how to reach each individual, and on and on. All aspects of leadership can be considered with one thought in mind: What would be expedient, as referred to in the scriptures? The Lord will determine what is best for us, lest we ask for something that would not be for our good.

After study, prayer, counsel, and gathering of all the best wisdom, you as a leader must come to some conclusion, then present your best reasoning to the Lord in prayer. Tell him what you plan to do, that which you "feel" is right. If it *is* right, you will feel a confirmation, a warm and peaceful feeling within.

Once you have that feeling, don't go back again and again for further reassurance. Have faith to act on the decision. If you reopen the decision without a good reason (such as the discovery of additional information, for example), it comes as an uncertain sound of the trumpet, and who shall prepare for the battle? (See 1 Corinthians 14:8.) An indecisive leader loses motivation, enthusiasm, support, and loyalty from followers. This doesn't mean you can't ever reconsider a decision, but such a practice should be the exception.

President Hinckley gives this wise counsel on decision making: "Deal with the problems as wisely as you can. Make your decisions. You may be right, you may be wrong. Hopefully you will be right because you have prayed earnestly over the matter and you have discussed it with your associates. But once made, put these decisions behind you and do not worry about them. Turn around, stand tall, put your head up, and look forward to the marvelous opportunities that you have" (*Teachings of Gordon B. Hinckley* [Salt Lake City: Deseret Book, 1997], p. 310).

We should not always expect an immediate answer to every inquiry. Sometimes we are to learn lessons through a test of our patience and our faith. The Lord says, "Dispute not because ye see not, for ye receive no witness until after the trial of your faith" (Ether 12:6). If we are keeping the commandments and our desire is to do right and we do not receive an immediate answer, we can proceed in faith, knowing that if the course chosen is contradictory to the Lord's will, he will make it known to us in due time. Some things we would like an answer to may not really matter; either choice would be all right. Our Father in heaven may be saying, "You decide."

My testimony of inspiration was reinforced in my mind after every open-house meeting we held at general conference time, when sisters from the Primary, Young Women, and Relief Society would meet together to refocus on the goals of their respective organizations and get clarification of guiding princi-ples. Without exception, leaders from local Church units would come up after presentations with excitement and enthu-siasm to report: "What was presented today was exactly the area we have been addressing in our planning meetings. We heard some of the same things we've been talking about in our stake or ward." And why wouldn't this be the situation? All true inspiration comes from the same source, and when there is a general need for answers, the inspiration falls like gentle rain on everyone who asks, seeks, knocks, and prepares the heart and mind to receive. There is a feeling of oneness, unity, and divine direction among all those seeking to know the Lord's will.

FRUITS OF THE SPIRIT

If we enumerate the fruits of the Spirit as attributes of Christlike leadership, we might evaluate our spiritual growth as we consider these attributes spoken of in Galatians 5:22–23: "But the fruit of the Spirit is love, joy, peace, longsuffering, gentleness, goodness, faith, meekness, temperance." When we experience these feelings within our hearts and minds, we can know that the Spirit is present. As leaders, let us pray to receive the Spirit, live to feel the Spirit, repent to keep the Spirit, and study to understand the Spirit.

I testify to you that through your obedience to God's com-mandments, you will become acquainted with the whisperings of his Spirit. In response to your asking, you will know and feel in your heart when to lead, when to follow, and when to turn away. You will be guided in every important decision. This I know to be true.

CHAPTER THIRTEEN

STAYING IN TUNE
AND IN TOUCH

And charity suffereth long, and is kind, and envieth not,
and is not puffed up, seeketh not her own, is not easily
provoked, thinketh no evil, and rejoiceth not in iniquity
but rejoiceth in the truth, beareth all things, believeth
all things, hopeth all things, endureth all things.

MORONI 7:45

My sister Sharon Larsen, while serving as stake Relief Society president some years ago, felt concern for what appeared to her a lack of connecting and caring among some of the sisters. She adapted the account of the Good Samaritan traveling on the road to Jericho to express her concern:

"A certain sister went down from her home to the local grocery store and fell among thieves who stripped her of her self-esteem and wounded her when she overheard them talking about her; and they caused her to suffer, leaving her heartbroken.

"And by chance, there came down that way a certain sister in fine clothes, and when she saw her she passed by without speaking.

"And likewise, a community leader, when she was at the store, came and looked on her and passed down by another aisle.

"But a certain sister, as she journeyed, came where she was, and when she saw her she had compassion on her and went to her and bound up her wounds by putting her arm around her and saying, 'Let's go talk for a while.'"

Talking with each other in love and tenderness and understanding is part of ministering, and ministering is at the heart of leadership. It is the lifeblood. It can change hearts, bring comfort to troubled hearts, heal wounded hearts, and make happy hearts. Opportunity must be provided for communication and camaraderie if we are to keep connected. However, simply meeting together does not necessarily bring people together in heart and soul.

As leaders traveling on our Jericho roads, even as good Samaritans, communication that puts us in touch and in tune with our sisters is so very, very important. It is quite possible to be within reach, even sitting side by side on the same bench, and yet be out of touch. We may talk to each other but not with each other. We may even look at each other but not see each other. While we may be busily engaged, even consumed with the responsibility of running programs, if we lose track of the individual, our efforts will be for naught.

I learned of a group of young women some time ago who were discussing a service project. But they weren't talking of painting houses or mowing lawns, as worthwhile as those activities may be. The Laurel class president, new to her calling and sensing the weight of her responsibility as a leader among her peers, pointed out to the girls: "We have Maria who belongs to our class and she hasn't been out for two months. Furthermore, her family doesn't even know where she is. For two months she has been a missing person." This young leader, who might have been looked upon as only a child, said, "Why don't we pray for her?" Another girl said, "Why don't we pray for her and fast for her?" A third added, "Why don't we all write to her?" The Young Women leader, who later confessed that sometimes we grown-ups lose some of our childlike faith, explained to the girls, "We don't know where she is. We don't know where to send the letters." But she went on to support the young women by saying, "We will go as far as we can." So they fasted and prayed and wrote letters and sent them to the girl's home.

Should it be a surprise that a call came shortly thereafter from a family member, reporting, "Maria has called home. We know where she is. She is coming home." Do you think it made any difference to that girl that there were letters from her peers waiting for her, carrying the message that she was wanted and loved? The leader reported that Maria showed up at school the following Tuesday for the first time in two months. Is it possible that the fervent, earnest prayers of an anxious family in behalf of a precious child might have been answered through the inspiration given to a young leader who was in tune and in touch with the needs of her sisters? Surely this is the Lord's way.

In the pioneer era, the camaraderie that was forged during those times of trial and tribulation was often described as the community of the Saints. They had a lot of togetherness. They needed each other. They walked together, side by side, mile after mile, day after day. They depended on each other as they traveled together, camped together, and suffered together. They sang together. Their hearts were knit together as they struggled for survival.

Our era is different. In fact, it is so different that we can live almost in isolation of one another. Our schedules and time commitments are not conducive to talking over the back fence, or picking berries together, or sitting around the quilting frames. Today many in our society express a sense of loneliness even while rushing here and there. Yes, things have changed, and in some cases that is good. But if the warmth, the comforts, the luxuries of our homes, the modern technology that permits us to be connected electronically with the world, and the socialization with the personalities on TV keep us from being in tune and in touch with each other, we have suffered a terrible loss.

That camaraderie of the early Saints is still needed today, not necessarily in the same way, but with the same result. In the absence of communication that allows us to be in touch with one another, we are prone to make judgments based on detached observations. We may miss entirely the understanding that would allow us to reach out in a helpful way as sisters.

Just for illustration, imagine that a young woman in your ward has walked into the chapel a little late for sacrament meeting and taken a seat on the back row. It is obvious that she has tears in her eyes. You as her leader might make a quick observation. Perhaps your first impulse is to offer help. However, ministering often begins with listening. Before you attempt to "fix the problem," you might try to gain more understanding.

Why might she be crying? The answers could range from losing her boyfriend to arguing with her mother to having a bad hair day to slamming her finger in the car door. Maybe she just had a wonderful spiritual experience that filled her eyes with tears. If you are to minister to her needs, would the appropriate attention be to apply a Band-Aid, seek a priesthood blessing for her, or just listen to and understand her? Observing what people are doing may be the least effective method of getting to know and understand those we would lead and love.

The Lord didn't say to just count the sheep, to see if their names were on the roll. He said, "Feed my lambs." The following illustration, known as the Awareness Wheel, indicates the need to look beyond what people are doing and find what they are needing, if we truly want to minister to one another. This wheel is divided into five different segments: Doing, Feeling, Needing, Wanting, and Interpreting. We tend to use the segment "Doing" almost to the exclusion of the others. We observe what people are doing and respond to that small segment, which may reveal the least valid information concerning what a person may be feeling or wanting, interpreting or needing.

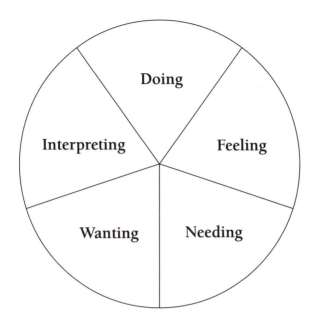

The consequence of responding to only what we observe may cause us to turn away at the very time we should reach out. This is sometimes the case with sisters whose actions give the impression that all is well. But walking side by side for only a brief time would reveal that the feeling of being needed and included is bone-marrow deep within all of us. And the appearance that all is well on the outside may in fact be covering an aching heart deep within.

I observed a wonderful example of a leader "looking deeper" one Sunday morning on Vancouver Island in British Columbia. The Relief Society meeting had just begun. A sister who appeared timid, with her head down, slipped in a minute or two late and took a seat on the back row by the door where I was sitting. I didn't recognize her, but I whispered a brief greeting, and she responded, "I'm new in the ward." In that setting I witnessed leadership at its best. The ward choir leader was given a few minutes to announce a special choir rehearsal that was to be held in preparation for the upcoming ward conference. She acknowledged the new sister on the back row and extended an invitation: "Would you join us?" The sister beside me just shook her head and timidly responded, "You don't want me in your choir; I don't sing."

This great leader who was responsible for the musical presentation at ward conference was looking beyond the choir when she said with enthusiasm, "Can you start on time and stop on time, when I give the signal?" The sister nodded her head affirmatively, and the choir director said, "You're in."

I learned later that this dear sister, new in the ward, had not been to church for quite some time. "Less active" would have been her designation in people's minds. But when the leader of the choir, who was also a leader of people, said, "You're in," this sister whispered to me, "I've never been in before."

A little thing? Not so. Really, a very big happening of eternal consequence took place in this brief exchange. Suppose the choir director had made a judgment based on what she observed: a sister coming in late, taking a seat on the back row, and keeping her head down. The story might have stopped there, and furthermore, the sister's attempt to return to the fold might also have stopped.

A choir leader, yes, but also a leader of sisters was in tune and in touch with a sister's heart, regardless of her words. And this sister, at least while I was in the area, moved from the less-active role to join those who were "in."

It is as we have opportunities to spend time together, to sing together, to serve together, and to look at one another that our hearts are opened and we come to know what a person is feeling, interpreting, wanting, and needing. The shy woman on the back row, for instance, had clearly suffered from feelings of being left out. Perhaps she had interpreted the silence of others in previous settings as intentional shunning. She wanted and needed to be included.

When we build relationships of trust, we are better prepared to "bear one another's burdens, that they may be light; . . . and are willing to mourn with those that mourn; yea, and comfort those that stand in need of comfort, and to stand as witnesses of God at all times and in all things, and in all places" (Mosiah 18:8–9). We then begin to follow the admonition of the Savior, "A new commandment I give unto you, That ye love one another; as I have loved you, that ye also love one another" (John 13:34).

The Church provides us many opportunities to be in tune and in touch: visiting teaching, working at the cannery, attending homemaking meetings, participating in activities, worshiping together. If "small talk" is the extent of our conversation at such times, we may still be strangers although we may have traveled together side by side for months and even years.

One year at Christmastime all the sisters in our ward were invited to a Relief Society gathering at a neighbor's home. Although the ward had been recently divided and many sisters were getting acquainted for the first time in a social setting, still there were many who had been longtime neighbors, who had waved to each other every time they went up and down the street and of course at church and the grocery store and wherever their paths crossed. They would certainly consider themselves friends. It was a delightful, fun party, with smiles and laughter and certainly an "all-is-well" atmosphere.

I had been asked to present a Christmas message at the close of the festivities. It seemed to me that if we could give each other gifts of love, real love that could be felt and remembered and taken home in our hearts, then surely that would be the Christmas message for all seasons. And furthermore, that love would come as a gift from the heart of each one present.

I had participated in an activity several years before that had touched my heart and helped me sense the difference between just talking and being in touch. Sharing that experience, I felt, would be appropriate on this occasion and help me accomplish one of the main purposes of the evening.

So I asked each sister to find a partner, it didn't matter who, someone they knew well or not so well. I explained that we were going to talk with each other. I would tell them what to talk about, and when I gave the signal, they were to stop talking and listen for the next instruction. They were in a happy mood, and I knew that getting a conversation going would be no challenge; maybe stopping it when I signaled would be a bigger one.

I instructed them to stand and put their hands together—one sister with both palms raised and the other sister with her palms laid on her partner's hands. Since the partners were to take turns talking as directed, the one whose hands were on top would speak to her partner first, and then they would switch places with their hands and the other partner would take her turn.

There was much laughter and merriment as everyone got into position and prepared to follow further instructions. The first assignment was for each sister to say three things about herself and three things about her partner that might be classified as "small talk." For example, one might say about herself, "I like ice cream," and about her partner, "I like your blouse." This is small talk. Whether recipes, foods, or fashions were being shared, the response was laughter and even a little noise.

Once I got the sisters' attention from their one-on-one conversations, I explained the next step. They were to keep their hands together, each taking turns talking as before. But this time each sister was to share something with her partner that she really valued, something really important to her, something that really mattered. The conversation began immediately. It was interesting to note that the noise level was somewhat subdued.

After allowing time for this one-on-one communication about something each one really valued, again I got their attention, this time by playing a chord on the piano because they were so involved. I proceeded with the next instruction. They were to talk together—not necessarily taking turns or having their hands together—just to talk with each other about anything they would be willing to work on together to make a contribution to some worthwhile project in our ward. The conversation began again, with women sharing thoughts and ideas freely as they came. After only two or three minutes, I stopped the conversation. There seemed to be a universal reluctance to stop talking, but they responded.

The next instruction was to put their hands together once again, taking turns as they had before, and share with their partners something that gave them concern—maybe a worry or a burden or a feeling of unrest, not too personal, of course, but something that was heavy on their minds. The sharing began. The tone of the voices was lower. After only a brief time, many were embracing each other. Some even had tears in their eyes. A spirit of love and concern seemed to permeate the room. It was quieter. It seemed to me that the Christmas tree in the corner took on a different glow. After a few minutes I signaled for their attention once again.

This time I gave no instruction about having hands together, I simply said, "In the next two or three minutes, would each of you express to your partner what message you would want to give if you knew this was the last time you would ever see her in this earth life." There was a pause. Voices were low. I couldn't hear what was being said, but many more partners embraced each other and many had eyes filled with tears. As the sisters took their seats, a feeling of tenderness prevailed. They were in touch and in tune, heart to heart, filled with love for each other.

I then asked the sisters to try to understand what had happened in so short a time, what they felt and why. They had gone far beyond the "doing" segment of the Awareness Wheel and observed what others were feeling, needing, wanting, and interpreting. We walked through each step of the exercise, seeking understanding.

At first, the communication was on the level of simple small talk. You might call it breaking the ice. This is the level of much of our conversation week after week as we sit together but don't really get together. The next step was to share something of value. This level of conversation begins to invite a level of trust. We talk about things that matter. The next objective was to not take turns, as in "you" and then "me," but to share something the partners would work on together, which makes them "us." This step was followed by one that is sometimes a bit of a risk: to share something that is a concern, a burden. This is especially hard when in our society we always want to appear as if all is well. Heaven forbid we should acknowledge that we have a burden! But how can we help carry one another's burdens if we don't know one another well enough to share our feelings?

It was observed that at this point many sisters began spontaneously embracing each other, a natural response when we feel the sincerity of someone's concern. This might be called bonding or connecting; it is truly being in tune and in touch with each other and with the Spirit. When we feel the Spirit, we feel love. And finally, after such tender feelings had surfaced and they were to express a farewell message, there was a realization, a discovery of deep feelings of love for one another.

A few with tears in their eyes were willing to share with the group what they felt, what they said, and what had happened. One older sister who was revered in our neighborhood was partnered with a younger sister; they had known each other for years. The younger sister told of how she had always felt she had not been accepted by the older sister for some reason she did not understand. On this occasion, in the atmosphere of feeling safe, she expressed this to the older sister. Her partner was very surprised and very concerned, since she had felt such admiration and love for this younger sister but had never taken the opportunity to express her feelings. There had been a misperception for years. They stood together in an embrace that touched all our hearts as we witnessed the power of love.

This group of sisters, real sisters, then stood together and sang "As I Have Loved You." We lingered, feeling a bond of sisterhood that will long be remembered and is often referred to. Several sisters expressed the feeling that the person they happened to team up with turned out to be not a coincidental choice at all. Miracles can happen when we are in touch.

Now, of course, this kind of activity is not necessary for this feeling of love to develop. In fact, it serves only as an example of what can happen any time and every time we decide to talk about things that are more important than the weather. When we are sharing messages of importance and learning of each other's values, our communication is more than just talking. We are on the Lord's errand. We experience and participate in the commandment to love one another as he has loved us.

In the words of President Spencer W. Kimball: "Jesus said several times, 'Come, follow me.' His was a program of 'do what I do,' rather than 'do what I say.' His innate brilliance would have permitted him to put on a dazzling display, but that would have left his followers far behind. He walked and worked with those he was to serve. His was not a long-distance leadership. He was not afraid of close friendships; he was not afraid that proximity to him would disappoint his followers. The leaven of true leadership cannot lift others unless we are with and serve those to be led" (*Ensign,* August 1979, p. 24). May we similarly stay in tune and in touch with those we are privileged to lead, guide, and walk beside.

CHAPTER FOURTEEN

MAGNIFYING OUR CALLINGS

For behold, it is not meet that I should command
in all things; for he that is compelled in all things,
the same is a slothful and not a wise servant;
wherefore he receiveth no reward.

D&C 58:26

As Latter-day Saint women, our greatest call to leadership begins in the home, but we must extend our sphere of influence as we reach out in the great cause of righteousness. A call to leadership in this cause is unlike leadership responsibilities in any other circumstances. Our cause is different. The system is different. The outcome is different. We understand and accept procedures foreign and even peculiar to the world. For example, a sister told me with some excitement that her husband had been recently released after serving seven years as bishop, and now she and her husband had been called as leaders in the nursery. She continued, "And he loves it. The children love him and he is magnifying his calling."

Imagine a bishop, a leader in the public view, presiding over a congregation, with power and authority to make decisions that affect an entire ward—now finding himself in one of the smaller rooms with the little children in the nursery. Does that make sense? How would this system be accepted or explained in a graduate class on leadership at the Harvard Business College? In the Lord's way, sometimes the most experienced are called to feed the lambs in the nursery, and the least experienced are called to reach and stretch beyond their comfort zone. As Elder Neal A. Maxwell explains: "A new calling beckons us away from comfortable routines wherein the needed competencies have already been developed" (*Ensign,* November 1995, p. 24).

When my sister Sharon was young and inexperienced but strong in faith and dedication, she was called to be the stake Young Women president. She was living with my husband and me at the time, and I clearly remember her concern over all she didn't know. She was following a very seasoned, mature, and successful leader. She explained, "I'm so young. I'm inexperienced. I have so much to learn." Many years later, as she was recently called as a counselor in the general Young Women's presidency, she confided to me: "I'm inexperienced. I have so much to learn." That is how it is with leadership the Lord's way. We learn and practice and accept different callings and continue a deep sense of feeling, "I have so much to learn."

FEELINGS OF INADEQUACY

As leaders we will have many humbling experiences that may cause us to question our ability. This is particularly so when we receive a new calling in which we have had little or no experience and where so much is expected. While an attitude of humility (being teachable) is most desirable to retain and cultivate, constantly questioning our ability is not.

Even tiny drops of water steadily dropping on a solid rock can cause a crack and eventually split the rock. Continual doubts about our ability are actually an indication of lack of faith, and can be destructive of the very gifts waiting to be magnified. As we move forward in faith, not fear, we magnify our gifts and our callings.

President Gordon B. Hinckley explains: "The Church will ask you to do many things. It will ask you to serve in various capacities. We do not have a professional ministry. You become the ministry of this Church and whenever you are called upon to serve, may I urge you to respond and as you do so, your faith will strengthen and increase. Faith is like the muscle of my arm. If I use it, if I nurture it, it grows strong; it will do many things. But if I put it in a sling, and do nothing with it, it will grow weak and useless and so will it be with you. If you accept every opportunity, if you accept every calling, the Lord will make it possible for you to perform it. The Church will not ask you to do anything which you cannot do with the help of the Lord. God bless you to do everything that you are called upon to do" (From member meetings in Praia, Santiago, and Cape Verde, Chile, February 22, 1998).

I learned to trust in the Lord early in my life when I received a report card in the sixth grade indicating that I had failed the grade. For me at that time, the experience reached far beyond the pain of having failed one grade in school. It became evidence to me that I was inadequate—or, as I put it, *dumb*—with no gifts, no talents, and no hope. A terrible word, *dumb*, and a terribly destructive thought. The fact that I had been out of school with illness for an extended period of time had no bearing on my feelings of failure.

This feeling of inadequacy that plagued me as a youth was reconfirmed in my junior year of high school when once again circumstances kept me absent from school enough to reflect seriously on my grades. Eventually, however, especially after I graduated from college, I felt quite assured that all those feelings were successfully left in the past. My favorite scripture had become my anchor: "Trust in the Lord with all thine heart; and lean not unto thine own understanding. In all thy ways acknowledge him, and he shall direct thy paths" (Proverbs 3:5-6). I had outgrown those childhood enemies that stood like Goliaths in my path—or so I thought.

But in subsequent years with each new calling, those seeds of doubt planted so early in my life would begin once again to sprout with enough evidence to raise concern. Reading a book on leadership by Elder Sterling W. Sill literally changed my perspective. In today's verbiage it would be called a "paradigm shift." It made a significant difference to my way of thinking. For those who may have or will experience these feelings of inadequacy, I share the words of Elder Sill:

"This idea of excelling in some trait was once mentioned

to a group of missionaries and after the meeting one rather skeptical missionary said, 'How could I excel in anything?' Then he proceeded to express the idea that in his opinion he had no talents worth mentioning. He more or less accused the Lord of passing him up when the gifts were distributed. That is the usual pattern of failure. One of our biggest sins is our own negation of our gifts. This trait we mistakenly think of as modesty or humility. This missionary was a fine young man of substantial potentiality, most of which was going to waste. It seemed never to have occurred to him that God was his father and had endowed him with all of his own attributes. All of his life this young man had greatly underestimated his own possibilities. He had accused God by his severe lack of faith in himself. Naturally his lack of effort at self-development and service had been in proportion to his lack of faith. He was sinfully taking the great gifts that the Creator had given him and destructively depreciating their value. The fault of not being aware of our own possibilities is very common, very destructive, and very sinful" (*Leadership,* 3 vols. [Salt Lake City: Bookcraft, 1958], 1:380).

The realization that focusing on my inadequacies might be considered sinful came as a wake-up call for me. These feelings of inadequacy are problems not to endure but rather to overcome; not once and for all but again and again, every time a seed begins to sprout. This is not something we do with self-help programs or positive-thinking seminars, although such resources may be helpful. It is not in our own strength but in the strength of the Lord, knowing and understanding the principle of grace, that we develop confidence, courage, and conviction.

There have been various times over the years when I have needed to conquer feelings of inadequacy that might have developed into fear, but never more than during an experience I had as general Young Women president. I had been asked by the Brethren to go to New York City (a long way from my hometown of three hundred people) and represent the Church before the National Pornography Commission.

On January 22, 1986, as I walked into the majestic, historic halls where laws are interpreted and justice is enforced, I was amazed at all the media present. This issue was a matter of national interest. The most powerful legal voices, representing magazines and filmmakers with large sums of money at stake, were prepared to present their case, calling upon the Fourth Amendment to justify the proliferation of this deadly sin. Opposing voices would also be given a hearing, and I was there to represent at least one strong opposing voice.

The panel of judges—twelve, as I recall—sat stern and seemingly indifferent while those in favor spoke boldly and arrogantly in defense of their position to spread their destructive product. This was not a time to ponder even for a split second any feelings I may ever have had of inadequacy. Such thoughts could have been fatal to my purpose for being there. It was a time to forget myself completely and trust in the Lord. I knew I was on his errand. I was there to voice a message that was in direct conflict with all that had been so blatantly presented thus far.

I recalled the promise of the Lord, "if ye are prepared ye shall not fear" (D&C 38:30). With the help of others, I had prepared the best I could in the brief amount of time given. It must not be in my ability but in the strength of the Lord that I would stand at the podium in that foreign environment and speak out. As I heard my name called representing The Church of Jesus Christ of Latter-day Saints, I stood up. And as I began walking forward, I felt a confidence, a boldness, a peace.

Forgetting myself and relying on the Lord, I stepped to the podium. "My name is Ardeth Kapp," I said. "I'm a Canadian by birth. More than three decades ago, in a solemn ceremony before an authorized magistrate in this free land of America, I raised my hand and took an oath of allegiance which I repeat in part: 'I hereby declare an oath . . . that I will support and defend the Constitution and the laws of the United States of

America against all enemies, foreign and domestic . . . and that I take this obligation freely. So help me God.'

"As a citizen of the United States and a member of The Church of Jesus Christ of Latter-day Saints, it is with alarm and a great sense of responsibility that I see an enemy invading our great country. I refer not to the overthrow of political territory, but a psychological warfare against the mind of man. I refer to the enemy of pornography, obscenity, and indecency. I speak on behalf of nearly six million members of The Church of Jesus Christ of Latter-day Saints, sometimes known as the LDS Church or the Mormons."

My voice did not waver and my knees did not shake and I did not stand alone. I delivered the message without fear. And although the voice of one may not have stemmed the tide of evil, there was no question that the representation of the Church and the message given, confirmed by the Spirit, was far more powerful than the messenger.

MAGNIFYING OUR TALENTS

Each of us has a stewardship responsibility to develop his or her gifts and talents. The parable of the talents indicates how the Lord will foreclose on unused talents while he multiplies and magnifies those that are accepted in gratitude and used to serve and bless others. Elder Neal A. Maxwell counsels, "We can make quiet but more honest inventories of our strengths, since, in this connection, most of us are dishonest bookkeepers and need confirming 'outside auditors'" (*Ensign*, November 1976, p. 14).

There are some questions we should think about and answer for ourselves: What gifts do I have? How does the Lord want me to use my gifts? Do I seek after the right gifts? Do I desire these gifts enough to intently pursue them? Am I ever displeasing the Lord because I do not recognize the gifts I have been given? Am I burying my talents in the ground? As we ponder these questions in a sincere desire to magnify our callings and be wise and grateful stewards, the words of President Spencer W. Kimball reassure us of our great possibilities:

"One of the great teachings of the Man of Galilee, the Lord Jesus Christ, was that you and I carry within us immense possibilities. In urging us to be perfect as our Father in Heaven is perfect, Jesus was not taunting us or teasing us. He was telling us a powerful truth about our possibilities and about our potential. It is a truth almost too stunning to contemplate. . . .

"Each of us has more opportunities to do good and to be good than we ever use. These opportunities lie all around us. Whatever the size of our present circle of effective influence, if we were to improve our performance even a little bit, that circle would be enlarged. There are many individuals waiting to be touched and loved if we care enough to improve in our performance" (*Ensign*, August 1979, p. 7).

The prophet Alma offers timely counsel on how to prepare for such success in leadership: "Yea, he that repenteth and exerciseth faith, and bringeth forth good works, and prayeth continually without ceasing—unto such it is given to know the mysteries of God; yea, unto such it shall be given to reveal things which never have been revealed; yea, and it shall be given unto such to bring thousands of souls to repentance" (Alma 26:22).

When this pattern for spiritual preparation is ongoing and continuous, the insights and inspiration needed for effective leadership are likewise ongoing and continuous. After a time, we begin to feel comfortable with what is expected, secure in our work, and familiar with the program and its language: CTR, PEC, PPI, CES, EFY, MTC, and so on.

This provides another opportunity in leadership experience. Although often we feel inadequate in new callings, sometimes we may be called to positions in which we may feel overqualified. Is it ever possible to be overqualified for any calling in this church if we sense the opportunity to magnify our calling, go the extra mile, and see the possibilities? Not when we keep our focus on the very purpose of our work, to bring souls unto Christ.

I remember the important lesson I learned when Heber, my husband, was called to be the stake video specialist immediately upon his release from serving as stake president for nine years. Shortly after his call to be video specialist, a Primary president called on a snowy afternoon and requested his services: "Would you come Saturday afternoon to the stake center and set up the TV and video machine and be there to show a Disney video to the Primary children?" The day was planned to include snow activities on the hill by the church building, winding down with the video at around four o'clock.

The day's activities were to begin at two o'clock. The former stake president arranged to be on hand at the start of the activity to see the children tumble, slide, squeal, laugh, and play in the snow. At the appointed hour, when the Disney video was to be presented, he turned the machine on for the children. They cheered, they squealed, they pointed at the screen, shouting, "That's me, that's me, that's me!"

The stake video specialist had spent the early afternoon capturing the children's activities on film, and now they were reliving the fun as they watched themselves and their friends. It was as though they had discovered themselves in a new and wonderful way. Now, years later, many still remember the snowy afternoon when they saw the best show ever. Was the video specialist overqualified for the service he performed? Was strengthening a child's sense of importance or worth or identity a minor calling? If we value a position or title more than an opportunity to serve, perhaps we are adopting the world's criteria for worth.

In a general conference session on April 9, 1951, I heard President J. Reuben Clark express these unforgettable sentiments: "In the service of the Lord, it is not where you serve but how. In the Church of Jesus Christ of Latter-day Saints, one takes the place to which one is duly called, which place one neither seeks nor declines" (Conference Report, April 1951, p. 154).

To receive a testimony of one's call puts all other concerns at rest. We want to know the Lord's will and we want to carry it out. If we know that a calling is the Lord's will, we can trust it is for our blessing and good. It is important to receive that testimony. If you don't feel that assurance at first, pray for that sweet feeling of peace that brings comfort to the spirit.

May we each go forth in faith, not fear, with gratitude for all that the Lord has given us, knowing that when we have done our best, by the grace of God he will do all the rest. May we learn to accept callings with humility and magnify them with all our strength, that those we lead, guide, and walk beside may be brought closer to Christ.

CHAPTER FIFTEEN

WORK HARD–PLAY HARD

*And see that all these things are done in wisdom and
order; for it is not requisite that a man should run faster
than he has strength. And again, it is expedient that he
should be diligent, that thereby he might win the prize;
therefore, all things must be done in order.*

MOSIAH 4:27

You might have been asked by neighbors or friends, as they
observe your comings and goings, your preparation time,
your meetings, your service, and your public and quiet labors,
"Why do you work so hard at your calling?" You might on
occasion even ask yourself the same question—after the last
phone call has been made; or the last item has been put away
following girls camp (for this year, that is); or the last assignment at the cannery has been accepted; or the weekly dinner
for the missionaries has been taken care of; or the special work-
shop for family history has been scheduled; or the visit to the
new move-in has been completed; or the Primary rehearsal for
sacrament meeting has had its final polish. Why do I do all
this? Why do I work so hard?

Work is the effort that makes what you want to have happen, happen. I learned this lesson years ago, in the days when
you couldn't run to the corner store to pick up several of your
favorite flavors of ice cream to be placed in the freezer. Today,
you can go at a moment's notice, select the flavor or flavors that
you like best, and instantly have your desire satisfied. Back
then, it took a long time and a lot of work before our desire for
ice cream could be realized. I have come to think of the process
as "the parable of the ice cream."

In the wintertime, the project for making ice cream began
with a trip to the nearby frozen river, where we would cut

blocks of ice to bring home in a big brown gunnysack. During the summertime, we would go to the icehouse by the barn, where we had stored ice during the winter for such an occasion. We retrieved this precious commodity from mounds of sawdust and carried it to the house.

As we worked to chop the ice into smaller chunks to be ready for the freezer, Mom would be preparing the filling for the ice cream. Our favorite flavor was caramel. It took considerable time to gradually brown the sugar until it became caramelized and then mix it with the cream that had been skimmed from the milk obtained from our Jersey cow. The filling was finally ready to be poured into the round metal container, which in turn was placed in the wooden, bucketlike freezer. The anticipation of the taste of ice cream began to be a reality at this point.

Next, the handle that rotated the paddlelike arms was fitted firmly in place. We had a small shovel to scoop the chunked ice into the freezer, but I remember grabbing handfuls of ice in my eagerness for the forthcoming delicacy, hoping to hurry the process as Dad carefully packed it firmly around the container.

When all was ready, the real work began. We took turns helping, according to our ability. I turned the handle first, and my older brother helped when the cream started to freeze and it became harder to turn. Toward the end, when even he had difficulty turning the handle, our dad would take over with considerable ease and keep it going. At this point I helped keep the freezer in place by standing with one foot on the top of the bucket and balancing myself with my hand resting on Dad's shoulder as he, on bended knee, leaned over the freezer. We waited and waited and turned and turned until the filling inside was so firm that even Dad could hardly turn the handle. We knew then that the job was done. It was an anxious moment.

The handle that had been turned so many times was taken off and set aside. We watched and waited in great anticipation as the lid was removed from the metal container. Mom came with a spoon for each of us and a pan to hold the paddle, and finally, that first spoonful of cold, sweet, wonderful caramel ice cream testified of the reward for all our work.

Satisfying the desire for ice cream is much easier nowadays, but the lessons learned in the process of making ice cream were far more lasting and more important than even the caramel ice cream itself. The relationships we built, the stories we told, the memories we made, the love we shared, and the common goal that kept us working together until the job was done bound us together in many more causes than the cause of ice cream. What we wanted to *do* was make ice cream and eat it, but what happened in the process was something far greater that has lasted longer and been more precious than even that first taste of that mouth-watering delicacy.

And now to the question, Why do we do all this? Why do we work so hard? Because it is impossible to measure the worth of all that is really happening while we're doing what we're doing.

Aesop tells a fable of a farmer who was about to die calling his sons around his bed to give them his last words. "My sons," he said, "my last legacy to you is a hidden treasure that is buried in our vineyard. If you will dig diligently to find it, you will become rich men." This was an irresistible opportunity, and as soon as their father was dead, the sons began their quest. They dug through the whole vineyard, turning over and breaking up the soil in their vain search for the treasure. They found no buried wealth, but the carefully spaded vineyard produced the richest crop it had ever brought forth. Aesop gives the moral of the story: There is no treasure without toil. I like to add to that the thought that sometimes the true treasure is different from what we had envisioned, but of no less worth.

There are various motivating factors that drive people to work. Some people may be motivated to work hard because of fear: fear of failing, fear of disappointing someone, fear of not being accepted if things don't measure up, fear of being embarrassed if things don't go right. Is it safe to say that we all have experienced some of those feelings somewhere along the way?

Some people are motivated to work hard because of a keen sense of duty. They are committed to accept responsibility. Duty drives them to be trustworthy and dependable. When duty calls, they hear the call and respond, "You can count on me." These people are a valuable strength to the building of the kingdom and can be found in wards and branches throughout the world. Fear and duty are both powerful motivators for working hard.

But the greatest motivation to work is a sincere sense of love. Love for the work. Love for the people. Love for the results. Love for the opportunity to serve. Love for the personal growth that comes. Love for the blessings of helping to build the kingdom. Love for the Lord. Love is the motivation that keeps us going until the work is done. And, as we learned in the parable of the ice cream, when the ice cream had become so hard that we children could no longer turn the handle, our father was there to finish the work. Without him we could have never accomplished our goal in spite of our love for ice cream.

A TIME FOR PLAY

King Benjamin gave great counsel regarding work: "And see that all these things are done in wisdom and order; for it is not requisite that a man should run faster than he has strength. And again, it is expedient that he should be diligent, that thereby he might win the prize; therefore, all things must be done in order" (Mosiah 4:27).

As leaders, we need to be sensitive to the needs of others and realize the benefits that come from occasions provided for rejuvenation, replenishment, revival, and repair. In the secular world, this kind of experience takes place in what is sometimes referred to as a "retreat." People get away from the office or work location, usually in an informal setting, to strengthen relationships, take a fresh look at things, explore creative ideas, and rekindle their enthusiasm for the work.

Elder Robert L. Backman, who was serving as Young Men general president during the time I was serving as Young Women president, agreed that the principle of retreats was sound, but there was something about the idea that never quite rang clear with him. When an occasion of this kind was deemed important, he was always in full favor, provided we dropped the term *retreat* and called it an *advance*. He would say, in his enthusiastic way, "In the work we are called to do in this church, we never retreat, we only advance."

Some years ago I learned about the benefits of pausing to celebrate our progress and become rejuvenated before pressing on further. The bishop of our ward, Dallas Bradford, had given me the assignment to get all the young men and young women in the ward to read the Book of Mormon within a specific period of time. We organized the youth in groups, with captains of ten. We had specific, measurable goals, and group members reported weekly to their captains.

The plan was good, but it was not until we identified what we called "Celebration Stations" at regular intervals along the way that the progress we had hoped for began to evolve. These were activities that allowed us to stop briefly in our responsibilities, evaluate our progress, rejoice with each other, and then move on. For example, when we all got through 1 Nephi, we had a Celebration Station. We organized a Liahona Hunt, using clues from scriptures to find the hidden treasure.

When we finished Alma 32, we put slips of paper with everyone's names into a piece of PVC pipe and buried the pipe among the roots of a young tree that we planted on the church grounds. This symbolized our united testimonies that would grow into a mighty tree: "And now behold, if ye nourish it with much care it will get root, and grow up, and bring forth fruit" (Alma 32:37).

When we finished the book of Alma, which required some work for everyone, we made a flag like the Title of Liberty, put all our names on it, and raised it on the flagpole in front of the church.

These Celebration Stations continued on through the project until the fun of it became so contagious that even the adults wanted to be organized with captains of ten. They called themselves "Alma the Olders." The anticipation of coming together to celebrate and cheer each other on kept the momentum and enthusiasm up until the goal was reached.

My father, who was a farmer who knew a lot about hard work and staying with a job until it was done, used to say in the heat of the day:

> *If you keep your nose to the grindstone rough*
> *And you keep it there long enough*
> *You will soon forget there are such things*
> *As the brooks that babble*
> *And the birds that sing*
> *Of these three things will your world compose:*
> *Just you, the grindstone, and your poor old nose.*

At the end of the day's work, the summer ritual of a swim in the river brought the refreshment and anticipation for yet another day's work.

Today there are those who go about their work with one ear turned to distracting music or TV programs. And there are also those who go out to play with a beeper and a cellular phone to keep them connected to their work. The following lines from our childhood McGuffy primer serve as a helpful reminder:

> *Work while you work, play while you play:*
> *One thing each time, that is the way.*
> *All that you do, do with your might:*
> *Things done by halves*
> *Are not done right.*
>
> (As quoted in The Book of Virtues, edited,
> with commentary, by William J. Bennett [New
> York: Simon and Schuster, 1993], p. 355)

We need time to work, and we need time to play. We also need leisure time to ponder and meditate and relax if we are to keep in tune with the Spirit.

Concerning the importance of time for meditation, President Harold B. Lee gave the following address: "A few weeks ago, President David O. McKay related to the Twelve an interesting experience, and I asked him yesterday if I might repeat it to you this morning. He said it is a great thing to be responsive to the whispering of the Spirit, and we know that when these whisperings come it is a gift and our privilege to have them. They come when we are relaxed and *not under the pressure of appointments.*

"The President then took occasion to relate an experience in the life of Bishop John Wells, former member of the Presiding Bishopric. A son of Bishop Wells was killed in Emigration Canyon on a railroad track. . . . His boy was run over by a freight train. Sister Wells was inconsolable. She mourned during the three days prior to the funeral, received no comfort at the funeral, and was in a rather serious state of mind.

"One day soon after the funeral services while she was lying on her bed, relaxed, still mourning, she said her son appeared to her and said, 'Mother, do not mourn, do not cry. I am all right.' He told her that she did not understand how the accident happened and explained that he had given the signal to the engineer to move on, and then made the usual effort to catch the railing on the freight train; but as he attempted to do so his foot caught on a root and he failed to catch the handrail, and his body fell under the train. It was clearly an accident.

"Now, listen. He said that as soon as he realized he was in another environment he tried to see his father, *but couldn't reach him. His father was so busy with the duties in his office he could not respond to his call.* Therefore he had come to his mother. He said to her, 'You tell Father that all is well with me, and I want you not to mourn anymore.'

"Then the President made the statement that the point he had in mind was that when we are relaxed in a private room we are more susceptible to those things; and that so far as he was concerned, his best thoughts come after he gets up in the morning and is relaxed and thinking about the duties of the day; that impressions come more clearly, as if it were to hear a voice. Those impressions are right. If we are worried about something and upset in our feelings, the inspiration does not come. If we so live that our minds are free from worry and our conscience is clear and our feelings are right toward one another, the operation of the Spirit of the Lord upon our spirit is as real as when we pick up the telephone; but when they come, we must be brave enough to take the suggested actions" (*The Teachings of Harold B. Lee* [Salt Lake City: Bookcraft, 1996], pp. 414-15; italics in original).

The need to work hard and also provide time for rest and relaxation is captured in the words of President Brigham Young: "Of the time that is allotted to man here on the earth, there is none to lose or to run to waste. After suitable rest and relaxation there is not a day, hour or minute that we should spend in idleness, but every minute of every day of our lives we should strive to improve our minds and to increase the faith of the holy Gospel, in charity, patience, and good works, that we may grow in the knowledge of the truth as it is spoken and prophesied of and written about" (*Discourses of Brigham Young,* comp. John A. Widtsoe [Salt Lake City: Deseret Book, 1975], p. 290). Adherence to this counsel will keep us from ever looking back in regret for what we might have done.

The scriptures remind us: "Be ye strong therefore, and let not your hands be weak: for your work shall be rewarded" (2 Chronicles 15:7). If we work hard and find time for play, we will be more effective leaders, better able to reap that promised reward.

CHAPTER SIXTEEN

A TIME TO BE RELEASED

*To every thing there is a season, and
a time to every purpose under the heaven.*
ECCLESIASTES 3:1

Just before my husband and I were to be released from our
leadership responsibilities in the Canada Vancouver
Mission, a dear sister in the ward asked me, "What are you
going to be when you return home?"

I hesitated a moment, and she further clarified her question, "I mean, what are you going to be doing when you're not
the Young Women president or the mission president's wife?
What will be your calling?" And then again she asked, "What
will you be?"

I thought for a while, not sure I had an answer to the question I felt she was asking. I finally responded, "I hope I will be
a good neighbor and a good member of the Church and probably a visiting teacher." She smiled, and the answer seemed to
satisfy her.

Elder Neal A. Maxwell reminds us: "It should be clear to us
with regard to various callings and assignments that just as
soon as we are sustained and set apart the clock begins running toward the moment of our release. How vital it is to manage our time and talents wisely from the moment a task begins!
Later, when we have devotedly invested much of ourselves in
a particular calling or assignment (and especially when it has
been satisfying and we have made a real difference), we may
feel the release when it comes, but that, too, is part of our
schooling as disciples. Being released gives us experience in
patience and humility, as well as a fresh reminder of our

replaceability" (*The Neal A. Maxwell Quote Book* [Salt Lake City: Bookcraft, 1997], p. 52).

At the time a call is made, there is inherent in the call the pending date for release. We usually are not given the exact day. It may not happen when expected, and it may not be easy when it does happen. It will usually come after we have formed close relationships, shared wonderful experiences, prayed together with associates in the work, and learned to serve and love. And we may think, Why couldn't it have been just a little longer?

My mind goes back to the time when President Gordon B. Hinckley informed Sister Patricia Holland that, after serving only two years in the Young Women general presidency, she was to be released. The prophet, of course, was aware of many other important things she was to do, but it seemed untimely to me. In response to our feelings, he counseled, "Don't be sad that it hasn't been longer. Be grateful that it happened at all." We must not look back, but always forward. We must not live in the past, for there is work to be done.

Sometimes a release from a calling can leave an emptiness. If our feeling of worth or importance in the Church is identified by a title that tells who we are, then when that title, that calling or position, comes to a close, we may feel a deep sense of loss. For some people, the lack of a calling or title that provides an easy identification might cause them to question their worth.

Looking back many years, I remember how I felt deep in my heart when a child came knocking on my door and asked if my children could come out and play. When I explained that I didn't have any children, the child put into words the question I had never dared ask, "If you're not a mother, what are you?"

If we're not identified by some "important" position or calling, do we still know who we are? At the time of a release, we may focus with greater understanding and appreciation on the title *sister* or, even more important, *daughter,* as in *daughter of*

God. Is that enough of an identification to give us a sense of worth?

Of course, there is a sense of loss anytime there is a change. You can't give your heart and soul to a calling and then walk away with no feelings or attachments or concern. If you could, one might wonder about your level of devotion to the calling.

One sister recently released from her calling as ward Relief Society president expressed to me a feeling of tremendous loss and emptiness. With tears in her eyes she said, "You just feel that mantle leave." She may have been recalling the spiritual support she had felt at the time she was set apart for her calling and sustained by the members of the ward as Relief Society president. She had been entitled to inspiration and revelation relating to that calling. She had undoubtedly had many experiences when the Spirit moved upon her on behalf of someone for whom she had a responsibility. And now that would not be the case. She wouldn't be entitled to the inspiration for that calling anymore. On the other hand, she wouldn't need it anymore. There is great order in the Lord's system of leadership.

However, it is important to remember and expect that inspiration and personal revelation will continue—not as they relate to a leader in the Relief Society but as they belong to every sister in the gospel. This assurance answers the question asked me by the sister in Canada: "What are you going to be?" The answer is stated very clearly in the Young Women theme, which applies to all women: "We are daughters of our Heavenly Father, who loves us, and we love him." That is who we are. And to the question, "What are you going to do?" the theme responds: "We will stand as witnesses of God at all times and in all things and in all places."

It is comforting to be reminded of the blessings that are promised to all faithful Saints, with or without a calling. Consider a prayer offered at the dedication of the Kirtland Temple: "And we ask thee, Holy Father, that thy servants may go forth from this house armed with thy power, and that thy name may be upon them, and thy glory be round about them, and thine angels have charge over them" (D&C 109:22). Can we ask for more of the Spirit to accompany us? If we are feeling a sense of spiritual loss after being released, might we be forgetting that there are other opportunities awaiting anyone who is willing to serve? We don't need an official calling to do family history work, perform temple endowments, visit the less active, comfort the sick, minister to the lonely, and on and on. An earnest prayer, "Where might I serve today?" will point the way.

We don't need a call to keep our covenants. In a revelation given to the Prophet Joseph Smith we read: "Verily I say, men [and women] should be anxiously engaged in a good cause, and do many things of their own free will, and bring to pass much righteousness; for the power is in them, wherein they are agents unto themselves. And inasmuch as [they] do good they shall in nowise lose their reward" (D&C 58:27–28).

The hymn title "We Are *All* Enlisted" reminds us that whether we have an official call to a specific assignment or not, still we are called to listen to the Spirit. We must all take part in the great conflict that began with the war in heaven and continues to rage here on the earth. Membership in the Church is itself a call to leadership, a call to lead out in the cause of truth and righteousness.

Some calls to serve come not from the bishop or the stake president, but rather from words or impressions the Lord speaks to us in our minds and hearts by the Holy Ghost (see D&C 8:2). In response to such a call, we may open our mouths and bear testimony to a neighbor or friend. We may lift another's load with expressions of love, or heal a wounded heart with a testimony of faith. We may offer resources of time and money, or take a stand in community causes that would enrich and protect the home. A "call" to unofficial service of this type is most often prompted by impressions that come to us personally, always in harmony with the principles and practices of the gospel. As members of the Church listening to the

Spirit we will receive many such calls, and each time we respond we will be anxiously engaged in a good cause.

A release from a calling does not erase our identity with the Lord, nor does it remove any of the good that has been accomplished during the time and season of our service. That remains and often grows, like seeds lying in fertile soil that blossom years later. But it frequently falls to others to harvest the garden we have helped plant.

This principle was impressed vividly on my mind during the October 1997 general conference. My younger sister, Sharon Larsen, had been called and sustained on Saturday as a counselor in the general Young Women presidency. Of course, I was pleased for her. As her sister, I had a ticket to the Sunday session on this important occasion. We decided to walk through the underground tunnel that leads from the Church Office Building to the Tabernacle.

I knew of the security measures in relation to that passageway. I had gone that way myself for eight years while serving as general Young Women president, although that had been a few years earlier. I felt comfortable. I thought I knew my way around, at least through the tunnel. It is hard to get lost in a tunnel. As we approached the entrance, the security officer was standing in his usual place, although it was a different officer than in previous years. At the gate he greeted Sister Larsen warmly, acknowledging her right to proceed on her way, and then turned to me and asked in a polite tone, "And who are you?" My sister vouched for me, saying, "She is my sister," and the man at the gate let me through.

After we moved along through the tunnel far enough to avoid being rude to the man who was carrying out his duty, we chuckled aloud. We talked of the lesson to be learned in that great experience. If I had still had the calling of president, the security officer would have known me. But I didn't have that calling anymore, and if Sharon had not been there, I would not have been allowed to enter. I had lost something besides my parking place in the garage.

Should this be of any concern? Not at all. Not really. We know from the words of the Lord through the scriptures, "Behold, the way for man is narrow, but it lieth in a straight course before him, and the keeper of the gate is the Holy One of Israel; and he employeth no servant there" (2 Nephi 9:41). We have the assurance that when we are called home there will be no question about our being recognized at the gate. The keeper of the gate will know us. Of that I am sure.

Our callings and titles and positions are not intended to bring us glory, but to bring glory to God. Should we ever lose the importance of that true principle, let the lines from the following poem ring clear:

The Torch Bearer

The God of the High Endeavor
Gave me a torch to bear
I lifted it high above me
In the dark and murky air;
And straightway with loud hosannas
The crowd proclaimed its light
And followed me as I carried my torch
Through the starless night,
Till drunk with people's praises
And mad with vanity
I forgot 'twas the torch they followed
And fancied they followed me.

Then slowly my arm grew weary
Upholding the shining load
And my tired feet went stumbling
Over the dusty road.
I fell with the torch beneath me.
In a moment the light was out.
When lo! from the throng a stripling
Sprang forth with a mighty shout,
Caught up the torch as it smoldered,
And lifted it high again,
Till fanned by the winds of heaven,
It fired the souls of men.

And as I lay in the darkness
The feet of the trampling crowd
Passed over and far beyond me,
Its paeans proclaimed aloud,
And I learned in the deepening twilight
This glorious verity,
'Tis the torch that the people follow,
Whoever the bearer may be.

(In Thomas Curtis Clark, comp., The Master of Men
[Freeport, N.Y.: Books for Libraries Press, 1970], p. 205)

We must pass the torch on. And when you do pass the torch on to another, and she carries the title you once had, you might ask her, as I asked my sister, "Be a little sensitive when you tell me rightly that things are better than they've ever been before." This church will continue to move onward and upward.

The time of a release is a time to feel, not emptiness, but the fulness of an abundant harvest. In the words of Luther Burbank: "Like the year at the end of summer, I pause now, toward the end of my allotted time, to glance backward and to gather my harvest of experience and growth and friendship and memory. And what has been my harvest of the years? As though they were the grains of the field, the fruits from the orchard and the flowers from the garden, bursting now with seed for another season, I seem to see three kinds of crops: the harvest of work accomplished and aims achieved, the harvested experience and lessons that have molded and impressed my life, and the harvest of dear friendships, happy memories. And the storehouse floor groans, and the walls bulge, and the shingles on the roof have to give a little to make room, for the harvest is rich and heavy and abundant."

CHAPTER SEVENTEEN

STAND UP, LEAD OUT

*Wherefore, ye must press forward with a steadfastness
in Christ, having a perfect brightness of hope,
and a love of God and of all men.*
2 NEPHI 31:20

President Gordon B. Hinckley has declared, "The time has come for us to stand a little taller, to lift our eyes and stretch our minds to a greater comprehension and understanding of the grand millennial mission of this The Church of Jesus Christ of Latter-day Saints. This is a season to be strong. It is a time to move forward without hesitation, knowing well the meaning, the breadth, and the importance of our mission" (*Ensign*, May 1995, p. 1).

At the great premortal council in heaven we "saw the Savior chosen and appointed and the plan of salvation made, and we sanctioned it" (*Teachings of the Prophet Joseph Smith*, p. 181). "The working out of the plan became . . . not merely the Father's work, and the Savior's work, but also our work" (John A. Widtsoe, *Utah Genealogical and Historical Magazine*, October 1934, p. 189). The Lord is counting on each one of us to do our part, wherever we are. To do this requires sorting through our lives and establishing our values, setting goals, and actually working toward salvation. It means making conscious, deliberate choices daily, even hourly, and having the moral courage to make our actions consistent with the path the Savior has shown. It means taking a stand, speaking up to defend those values we hold dear.

I take heart for the future when I consider examples such as this one from the experience of a nine-year-old boy. One day when his parents were away, by some devious means a *Playboy* magazine was delivered to the home. This child's sense of responsibility was deeply rooted in family values, teachings that inspired courage and confidence even when he was alone. He felt the need to lead out and take a stand. He sat down and wrote the following letter:

> Playboy,
>
> I think the free magzine you sent us was extremily un called for. I think that magzine you sent us was quite perverted. If you send another one I personally will take action.
>
> Thank you,
> Peter Olsen
> (not his real name)

The envelope was addressed with his return address, stamped, and ready to go when his parents returned. In a home where values are clearly taught and defended, leaders are born and trained.

We are called to contribute, to be accountable. This is not a time to ride the tide or to retreat. "They who are not for me are against me, saith our God" (2 Nephi 10:16). As we gain a greater sense of our mission and purpose in life, we find ourselves standing up and leading out.

A great example of moral courage to me is Joan of Arc. As I learned of her life, I was first of all impressed with her undying faith in the mission she believed she must fulfill. Her whole soul seemed to yearn toward God and her country. At the age of nineteen, she sealed her commitment when she was burned at the stake. In the play *Joan of Lorraine* by Maxwell Anderson, her words serve as an example of a young woman committed to her values: "I know this too now: Every man gives his life for what he believes. Every woman gives her life for what she believes. Sometimes people believe in little or nothing, nevertheless they give up their lives to that little or nothing. One life is all we have, and we live it as we believe in living it, and then it's gone. But to surrender what you are, and live without belief—that's more terrible than dying—more terrible than dying young" (as quoted in Ardeth Kapp, *Stand Up, Lead Out* [Salt Lake City: Deseret Book, 1990], p. 5).

As leaders in the Church, we may be willing to die for our cause. But we must also be willing to live for it. The Savior gave a beautiful parable to help us look to the future with joy and to be prepared for his second coming. In Matthew 25 he refers to himself as "the Bridegroom," and those who are preparing to come to the wedding celebration to meet him are represented by ten pure young women, the ten virgins. The wait is long, but then in the middle of the night, at the darkest hour, the joyous call is given: "Behold the Bridegroom cometh."

As leaders, will we be prepared to stand up and lead out? Will we be prepared to accept the invitation, "Awake and arise and go forth to meet the Bridegroom" (D&C 133:10)?

Consider the clarity of the call and the response of the brother of Jared when "the Lord said: Go to work and build," and "the brother of Jared did go to work, and also his brethren, and built barges . . . according to the instructions of the Lord" (Ether 2:16). Young Samuel likewise heard the call, and he responded, "Speak; for thy servant heareth" (1 Samuel 3:10). The call from the Lord to Mary was delivered by the angel Gabriel, and she responded with words of total trust, faith, and commitment: "Be it unto me according to thy word" (Luke 1:38).

Today prophets and apostles are giving a clear signal for us to stand up, speak out, and move forward. Callings in this church come from the Lord through revelation to his authorized servants. When we receive a call from the Lord through his designated priesthood leader, it won't matter whether it is to be a Primary teacher, a stake Relief Society president, or a Young Women leader. What matters is the Lord's counsel: "Be not weary in well-doing, for ye are laying the foundation of a great work. And out of small things proceedeth that which is great. Behold, the Lord requireth the heart and a willing mind" (D&C 64:33-34).

As women master the art of leadership, their impact is felt worldwide. In the teachings of Elder Neal A. Maxwell, we catch a glimpse of this enormous responsibility: "When the real history of mankind is fully disclosed, will it feature the echoes of gunfire or the shaping sound of lullabies? The great armistices made by military men or the peacemaking of women in homes and in neighborhoods? Will what happened in cradles and kitchens prove to be more controlling than what happened in congresses? When the surf of the centuries has made the great pyramids so much sand, the everlasting family will still be standing, because it is a celestial institution, formed outside telestial time. The women of God know this" (*Ensign,* May 1978, pp. 10-11).

President Spencer W. Kimball, reflecting on the influence of righteous women, declared: "Someday, when the whole story of this and previous dispensations is told, it will be filled with courageous stories of our women, of their wisdom and their devotion, their courage, for one senses that perhaps, just as women were the first at the sepulchre of the Lord Jesus Christ after his resurrection, our righteous women have so often been instinctively sensitive to things of eternal consequence" (*Ensign,* May 1978, p. 5).

We cannot stand on the sidelines and passively watch. We must stand up and lead out. As President Hinckley has said: "You are good. But it is not enough just to be good. You must be good for something. You must contribute good to the world. The world must be a better place for your presence. And the good that is in you must be spread to others. . . . In this world so filled with problems, so constantly threatened by dark and evil challenges, you can and must rise above mediocrity, above indifference. You can become involved and speak with a strong voice for that which is right" (*Teachings of Gordon B. Hinckley* [Salt Lake City: Deseret Book, 1997], p. 308).

May we as members young and old accept the challenge

and keep the faith. May we as women leaders catch the vision of leadership, learn the skills of leadership, and partake of the spirit of leadership. May we learn to be more effective in leading, guiding, and walking beside our family members, neighbors, colleagues, and fellow Saints, that we may truly defend the cause of our Lord now and in the future. May the Lord bless us all in our leadership responsibilities, is my earnest prayer for each one of us.

INDEX